Grace Pervades

David Hare has written nearly forty stage plays and over thirty screenplays for film and television. The plays include *Teeth 'n' Smiles*, *Plenty*, *Pravda* (with Howard Brenton), *The Secret Rapture*, *Racing Demon*, *Skylight*, *Amy's View*, *The Blue Room*, *Via Dolorosa*, *Stuff Happens*, *The Absence of War*, *The Judas Kiss*, *The Red Barn*, *The Moderate Soprano*, *Beat the Devil* and *Straight Line Crazy*. For cinema, he has written *The Hours*, *The Reader*, *Damage*, *Denial*, *Wetherby* and *The White Crow*, among others, while his television films include *Licking Hitler*, the *Worricker Trilogy*, *Collateral* and *Roadkill*. In a millennial poll of the greatest plays of the twentieth century, five of the top hundred were his.

by the same author

PLAYS ONE
(*Slag, Teeth 'n' Smiles, Knuckle, Licking Hitler, Plenty*)
PLAYS TWO
(*Fanshen, A Map of the World, Saigon, The Bay at Nice, The Secret Rapture*)
PLAYS THREE
(*Skylight, Amy's View, The Judas Kiss, My Zinc Bed*)

RACING DEMON
MURMURING JUDGES
THE ABSENCE OF WAR
VIA DOLOROSA
THE BREATH OF LIFE
THE PERMANENT WAY
STUFF HAPPENS
THE VERTICAL HOUR
GETHSEMANE
BERLIN/WALL
THE POWER OF YES
SOUTH DOWNS
BEHIND THE BEAUTIFUL FOREVERS
THE RED BARN
THE MODERATE SOPRANO
I'M NOT RUNNING
BEAT THE DEVIL
STRAIGHT LINE CRAZY
TEETH 'N' SMILES

adaptations
THE BLUE ROOM (from *La Ronde*) by Schnitzler
THE HOUSE OF BERNARDA ALBA by Lorca
ENEMIES by Gorky
YOUNG CHEKHOV (*Platonov, Ivanov, The Seagull*)
THE MASTER BUILDER by Ibsen
PETER GYNT after Ibsen

screenplays
COLLECTED SCREENPLAYS
(*Wetherby, Paris by Night, Strapless, Heading Home, Dreams of Leaving*)
THE HOURS

prose
ACTING UP
ASKING AROUND: BACKGROUND TO THE DAVID HARE TRILOGY
WRITING LEFT-HANDED
OBEDIENCE, STRUGGLE AND REVOLT
THE BLUE TOUCH PAPER
WE TRAVELLED

DAVID HARE

Grace Pervades

faber

First published in 2025
by Faber and Faber Limited
The Bindery, 51 Hatton Garden
London, EC1N 8HN

Reprinted in this revised edition 2026

Typeset by Brighton Gray
Printed and bound in the UK by CPI Group (Ltd), Croydon CR0 4YY

All rights reserved
© David Hare, 2025

David Hare is hereby identified as author
of this work in accordance with Section 77 of the
Copyright, Designs and Patents Act 1988

All rights whatsoever in this work, amateur or professional,
are strictly reserved. Applications for permission for any use
whatsoever including performance rights must be made in
advance, prior to any such proposed use, to
Casarotto Ramsay & Associates Ltd, 3rd Floor,
7 Savoy Court, Strand, London WC2R 0EX

No performance may be given unless a licence
has first been obtained

This book is sold subject to the condition that it shall not,
by way of trade or otherwise, be lent, resold, hired out
or otherwise circulated without the publisher's prior consent
in any form of binding or cover other than that in which
it is published and without a similar condition including
this condition being imposed on the subsequent purchaser

A CIP record for this book
is available from the British Library

ISBN 978-0-571-39361-9

Printed and bound in the UK on FSC® certified paper in line with our continuing
commitment to ethical business practices, sustainability and the environment.
For further information see faber.co.uk/environmental-policy

Our authorised representative in the EU for product safety is
Easy Access System Europe, Mustamäe tee 50, 10621 Tallinn, Estonia
gpsr.requests@easproject.com

4 6 8 10 9 7 5

Grace Pervades was first performed at Theatre Royal Bath, as part of the Ralph Fiennes season, on 27 June 2025. The cast was as follows:

Edward Gordon Craig Jordan Metcalfe
Edith Craig Ruby Ashbourne Serkis
Ellen Terry Miranda Raison
Henry Irving Ralph Fiennes

Kate Lewis / Clare Atwood Kathryn Wilder
Maid Harriet Leitch
Loveday Tom Kanji
Gertrude (Lyceum & Moscow) Jo Mousley
Christabel Marshall Helena Lymbery
Isadora Duncan Saskia Strallen
Claudius (Moscow) Damian Myerscough
Konstantin Stanislavski / Dr Mason Guy Paul
Leopold Sulerzhitsky Sharif Afifi

All other roles played by members of the company.

Director Jeremy Herrin
Set Designer Bob Crowley
Costume Designer Fotini Dimou
Lighting Designer Peter Mumford
Sound Designer Elizabeth Purnell
Composer Paul Englishby

Grace Pervades transferred to the Theatre Royal Haymarket, London, on 24 April 2026, with the following changes to the cast:

Gertrude Giulia Innocenti
Christabel Marshall Maggie Service
Claudius (Moscow) Chris Porter
Leopold Sulerzhitsky Youness Bouzinab

Understudies Sam Perry, Katherine Liley

Author's Note

Experts will recognise my departures from strict chronology which are, I hope, intentional. One of the pleasures of writing about these people is the huge and excellent literature they inspired. Especially valuable is Michael Holroyd's *A Strange Eventful History*. Ellen Terry's own *Memoirs* were edited by Christopher St John, who is portrayed in the play. No one can better Terry's description of her visit to Wolverhampton after Henry Irving's first collapse, when he looked 'like some beautiful grey tree that I have seen in Savannah'.

D.H.

For Nicole

Characters

Edward Gordon Craig
Teddy

Edith Craig
Edy

Ellen Terry

Henry Irving

Kate Lewis
née Terry

Maid

Gertrude

Claudius

Loveday

Clare Atwood
Tony

Christabel Marshall
Christopher St John

Isadora Duncan

Konstantin Stanislavski

Leopold 'Suler' Sulerzhitsky

Waiter

GRACE PERVADES

'Whether in movement or repose,
grace pervades the hussy.'

Charles Reade

Act One

1.

An empty stage, with music. Edward Gordon Craig, known as Teddy, arrives to address us. He wears an Edwardian suit.

Teddy And so. People often ask me 'What's it like being a genius?' I say, 'I don't know, because I've never been anything else.' I have no point of comparison.

I was always going to be remarkable. How could it be otherwise? My mother redefined the art of acting.

What was left for me to do? Simple. I redefined the art of theatre.

The music swells. On the opposite side appears Edith Craig, known as Edy. She is compact, neat, precise.

Edith People often ask me 'What's it like having a genius for a brother?' I say, 'I've no idea, I've never had one.' I've got one who keeps saying he's a genius, but that's not the same thing. To me, he's just little Teddy. Showing off, as usual.

My mother was the greatest actress in the history of England. That's why I was always determined to be ordinary.

The music swells again and a huge stage picture arrives showing the Rialto in Venice. Actors flow onto the stage in Venetian costume. At their centre, Ellen Terry appears, greeted by the raising of lights. She is in her thirties, fair-haired, with a supple athletic voice and immaculate phrasing. She is Portia in The Merchant of Venice.

Ellen 'The quality of mercy is not strained;
It droppeth as the gentle rain from heaven
Upon the place beneath. It is twice blessed:
It blesseth him that gives and him that takes:
'Tis mightiest in the mightiest; it becomes

The throned monarch better than his crown:
His sceptre shows the force of temporal power,
The attribute to awe and majesty,
Wherein doth sit the dread and fear of kings.'

Teddy shrugs at his mother's appearance.

Teddy Acting isn't of much interest. Not to me. If you're still an actor at forty, you need to ask yourself some serious questions.

Ellen 'But mercy is above this sceptred sway;
It is enthroned in the hearts of kings,
It is an attribute of God himself.'

Ellen turns away and the scene dissolves.

Edith Plays should exist for a purpose. Only when we have something to say. And a good, clear way of saying it. If you don't know why you're doing a play, don't do it. It will spare the audience a lot of needless suffering.

Teddy For a genius, the chances of being understood in England are zero. The only honourable course is exile. France is fine. France, Italy, Russia, they know about genius in Russia. And Germany, they're civilised in Germany. All right, the Nazi experiment didn't end well, but I'm happy to confess that at the beginning – yes, I supported it. I admired it. It was refreshing.

Edith Somebody once accused me of taking dull plays to dull towns. I said, 'I like that. Dull Plays to Dull Towns. That sums the Pioneer Players up perfectly. Can I use it in the advertising?'

The images turn to a Scottish castle realised in a Victorian pictorial style. Ellen turns, Lady Macbeth in Macbeth.

Ellen 'The raven himself is hoarse
That croaks the fatal entrance of Duncan
Under my battlements. Come you spirits

That tend on mortal thoughts, unsex me here
And fill me from the crown to the toe top-full
Of direst cruelty; make thick my blood,
Stop up the access and passage to remorse
That no compunctious visitings of nature
Shake my fell purpose, nor keep peace
Between the effect and it!'

Teddy turns back to us.

Teddy I've never seen my sister's work –

Edith I've never seen my brother's work – if there is any. Whatever he does, he does abroad where they love him. Or so he says.

Teddy They love me, they've always understood me.

Edith Teddy keeps saying fame is such a bother, but, honestly, Edward Gordon Craig could walk down Hawkhurst High Street entirely unmolested.

Teddy Edy just puts plays on. She takes some play – you know, written down – on the page – dead – and they all stand up and speak it. I don't call that theatre.

The image behind Ellen becomes Illyria – a place of fantasy. She is Viola, passionately addressing Olivia, in Twelfth Night.

Ellen 'Make me a willow cabin at your gate
And call upon my soul within the house;
Write loyal cantons of contemned love
And sing them loud even in the dead of night –'

Teddy All right, so we see things differently, my sister and I, but there is one thing we agreed on –

Ellen 'Halloo your name to the reverberate hills
And make the babbling gossip of the air
Cry out "Olivia" –'

Teddy That our mother was great, surpassingly great –

Edith And in all the years we lived, no other actress ever came near.

At once the music swells and overwhelms them all.

2.

Ellen and Kate Lewis (née Terry) are together in a comfortable sitting room in Kensington. There is a family resemblance. Ellen is thirty-one, Kate is a couple of years older and extremely beautiful. The year 1878 is projected.

Kate And so what do you think the reason is?

Ellen I have no idea.

Kate What is this fascination with Italy? Does anyone understand it?

Ellen No one I know.

Kate Padua. Messina.

Ellen Venice.

Kate Verona. Did he ever go there?

Ellen They say not.

Kate Then why did he set all his plays there? Here he is, the greatest poet in history –

Ellen Well, he doesn't know that yet, does he?

Kate And he decides, for some reason, not to write about England –

Ellen He does write about England –

Kate Yes, but not now. His now, I mean. He writes about England years before. Or about Italy.

Ellen I imagine he thought it was romantic.

Kate Italy?

Ellen Anything's better than England, don't you think?

Kate is disapproving.

Kate Ellen, I don't know where you gather such opinions. You have a weakness for fashionable ideas, which are unpatriotic.

Ellen I love my country, but I also see it. I promise you, having two children out of wedlock can do wonders for one's eyesight.

Kate Yes, but not for one's bank balance.

Ellen You notice nothing, Kate, because you're happily matched. Much the greatest thing about our country is its national poet. If I could choose a man for the rest of my life it would be William Shakespeare.

Kate Given your amorous record to date, that seems the safest option.

A Maid opens the door.

Maid A Mr Irving for you.

Kate Irving?

Maid Yes.

Kate We're not expecting any Irving.

Ellen Did he give his first name?

Maid No.

Ellen Did he seem like an actor?

Maid He seemed like a man in some trouble. As if something terrible had just happened unexpectedly.

Kate It's Henry Irving.

Maid He's in distress.

Ellen He's always in distress. It's fine.

Maid He's brought his dog.

Kate His dog is with him?

Maid At his feet.

Kate Show Mr Irving in.

Ellen But Charlie must stay in the hall.

The Maid goes out.

Did you invite Henry?

Kate Hardly. I don't know anyone who invites him socially.

Ellen He doesn't lighten the room, does he?

Kate Are you frightened of him?

Ellen Not in the slightest.

Kate Everyone else is.

Ellen I can't explain. Somehow, he never scared me.

Kate I must admit I always suspected him indifferent to me and to my gifts.

Ellen Well then, it transpires you're wrong. He can hardly have any other motive for calling.

Kate Doesn't he know I've retired?

Henry Irving comes in. He is around forty, with a thin leg which drags slightly. He is awkward with a deep voice, and an air of gravity.

Maid Mr Henry Irving.

Irving My goodness me, two birds, one stone. Two Terrys.

Ellen We thought it must be you, Mr Irving.

Irving You weren't expecting me?

Ellen Anything but.

Irving Forgive me, I sent word ahead.

Ellen We never received it. But that doesn't make you any less welcome.

Irving I'm thrown off my game.

Kate Don't be. Please. Sit.

The Maid goes. Irving seems anxious and stays standing.

Ellen I'm staying with my sister for a few weeks. She's with child.

Kate Again.

Irving I congratulate you. I'm delighted to hear it.

Kate So if you've come to talk about theatre, I'm afraid you'll be wasting your time.

Ellen Mr Irving talks about little else in my recollection.

He shifts a little.

I don't mean it unkindly.

Irving I don't take it unkindly.

Ellen You must be the most single-minded man I've ever met.

Irving I will take that as a compliment.

They all smile.

I admit I've played around seven hundred different roles –

Ellen Always in the provinces?

Irving Mostly in the provinces.

Ellen And you're still only forty –

Irving Sadly, I'm forty-one.

Irving waits a moment, knowing they expect him to speak.

Yes, seven hundred characters under my belt. I specialise in kings, counts, noblemen and princes. In Edinburgh I learned a new part every two days for seven hundred and sixty-two days. It would be more impressive if quantity were quality. But so be it. When I play one, I think of the next. Life passes in perpetual preparation. I've tried diligently to interest myself in other activities. I hope I give a passable imitation of an averagely curious person. I enjoy the company of my sons. But I'm irresistibly drawn back by the feeling that one day I may do it better than anyone else. Act, I mean. I have an aptitude. It would be sad to die without having used it to the full.

The words hang in the air for a moment.

Ellen My, my, that's certainly the longest speech I've heard you make –

Irving I'm sorry –

Ellen Not written by others, anyway – and the most passionate.

Kate smiles to herself.

Kate If I can ask you a direct question, Mr Irving –

Irving Please –

Kate I've heard rumours you're starting a new company.

Irving Correct. A Utopian company. A company of equals in which I am the boss –

Kate smiles to herself.

Kate I understand that you've been forced into management because you've fallen out with Mrs Bateman.

Irving The subject is indelicate and difficult to discuss openly. With ladies.

Kate We're quite robust –

Irving I don't doubt it –

Kate My sister prides herself on being bohemian.

Irving I remember.

Ellen I can withstand a little indelicacy, it's true. My personal history is not without blemish.

Irving Quite.

Kate We know you were employed by Mrs Bateman –

Irving I was.

Kate And it was said that she was pressing her daughter upon you.

Irving Pressing. Yes. Good word.

Irving stops a moment. Kate's enjoying herself.

I warned you the subject was indelicate. She wanted her daughter to take on the role of Ophelia.

Kate And you resisted?

Irving It appeared her daughter's interest was both professional and personal.

Ellen Goodness me.

Irving I'm a married man. I had to say no.

Kate And how did Mrs Bateman react?

Irving This is the curious thing. Her response was to walk away and to give me the lease.

Kate Of the theatre?

Irving Yes.

Kate For nothing?

Irving For the next few years. As a gift.

There is a slight pause.

Mrs Bateman is very generous.

Kate It's the Lyceum?

Irving The Lyceum, yes.

Kate It's a rat trap.

Irving You could say.

Kate Exactly how generous is that, then?

Irving In the right hands it will prosper. It needs love.

Kate You're taking over a disfavoured house.

Irving Hitherto disfavoured. I hope my *Hamlet* will improve its fortunes a little.

He smiles, self-deprecating.

Kate I understand why you're here, Mr Irving. But I have to warn you I'm extremely happy in my new life. I find motherhood intensely rewarding.

Irving I'm sure it is.

Kate In the circumstances you'll understand I'm not available.

Irving That is regrettable. But I have to confess I didn't come here to employ you.

Kate No? Then what exactly are you doing here?

Irving Why, to contract your sister.

Kate My sister?

Ellen Me?

Ellen looks genuinely amazed. Irving continues to speak to Kate.

Irving Yes. I don't mean to give offence.

Kate You haven't.

Ellen You want me?

Irving You needn't sound so surprised.

Ellen I've always lived in my sister's shadow. And I have always been happy there. There is a reason Kate is so admired.

Irving Nevertheless.

He waits. Ellen is disconcerted.

Ellen From childhood it's always been understood. There were eleven of us. Kate was always the most beautiful. And the most talented. She played Cordelia at fourteen. Extremely well.

Kate Thank you, sister.

Ellen And she is far better liked by the public than me. I've never regarded myself as a serious actress. My feeling is more for the visual arts. I like painting, drawing, sculpture.

Kate The father of her children was an artist.

Ellen Kate is the talented one.

Irving She is also retired.

Ellen So am I.

Irving Retired? And appearing at the Theatre Royal Holborn?

Ellen That's a favour. To a friend.

Irving Am I not a friend?

Ellen I was living in the country. Alone. I will be frank: I have Edy, and I have Teddy. Their father left me for a nineteen-year-old. I had nothing but a dirty cottage and a few chickens. We ate eggs at every meal. Yes, I was persuaded to accept a couple of acting engagements, but only because I was stony broke. You need to act, Mr Irving. I don't. I prefer to live.

Irving And you think the two are incompatible?

Both Kate and Irving are scrutinising her now, not convinced.

We did appear together once, remember.

Ellen And deeply unimpressive we were.

Irving That was hardly our fault. The play was by Garrick.

Ellen *The Taming of the Shrew,* rewritten.

Irving Rewritten? Rehashed. A stupid play to begin with and made stupider by Garrick's interventions. Who thinks it's funny to be rude to women?

Ellen It's a popular entertainment.

Irving Not in our hands, it wasn't.

Ellen You were nearly as bad as me in that play.

Irving Not quite.

Ellen So why do you want me now?

Irving looks down, in pain.

And I know what you will be offering.

Irving Financially?

Ellen No. Not financially. Artistically. All those awful Desdemonas, and Ophelias, who either weep or go mad. Cordelia. 'I love your majesty according to my bond; no more nor less!' One scene and then sit in the dressing room all night. No. They're all second fiddle. Drippy girls. Rosalind's the only one worth tuppence.

Irving It won't all be Shakespeare.

Ellen But that's where your heart is.

Irving And yours? Where is your heart, Miss Terry?

Ellen doesn't reply. Irving nods slightly, as though he had expected this evasion.

I have been thinking about my leading lady for months. You are my only possible choice.

Ellen Why?

Irving Why?

Ellen Yes. Why?

Ellen is getting irritated.

And whatever you do, don't say my charm, because whenever people refer to my charm, I become enraged.

Irving No cause. Very few people possess charm. I certainly don't.

Ellen Yes, but charm is a natural quality. It's something you're born with.

Kate Ellen would like to think she also possesses skill.

Ellen Whenever I do appear on a stage, people say, 'Oh she's so natural,' as if I were making no effort. It infuriates me.

Irving Quite.

Ellen 'She floats,' they say.

Irving I've heard that said.

Ellen They don't seem to realise floating is a technique.

Irving That's interesting.

Ellen If you want the trick of it, I do it by flicking the balls of my feet.

Irving Ah, the mystery laid bare!

Ellen 'She's at one side of the stage,' they say, 'and then suddenly she's at the other.' I don't get there by magic, you know.

Irving It must have taken hours of practice.

Ellen Have you read Nietzsche?

Irving Never.

Ellen 'All divine things run on light feet.' Now I put in just as much effort as anyone else, but I aim to excel at not letting it show.

Irving That's commendable.

Ellen Thank you. I don't regard actors who sweat and spit as especially accomplished. Grunting and heaving. That kind of behaviour belongs more properly on a building site.

Irving I will never praise your charm again. However.

He waits. Kate watches.

It is the potential contrast which attracts me.

Ellen You'll have to explain, Mr Irving.

Irving How do I put this? I am by nature atrabilious –

Kate Really?

Irving I know it is sometimes said that I have an overly heavy presence.

Ellen Have you heard that, Kate?

Kate Have I? Let me think. A heavy presence, you say?

Irving Something happens.

Ellen When?

Irving When I walk on stage.

Ellen What sort of thing?

Irving In my head, everything is speed and deftness. But then when I reach the stage, I become less speedy. And less deft. I will be frank. My critics accuse me of being dour.

Ellen Dour?

Irving Dour, yes. I'm drawn to tragedy – I prefer it, that's my character – but when I fail, I achieve only melancholy. An evening in my company can on occasions be very grim.

Ellen Onstage, you mean?

Irving Certainly onstage. Where else?

Kate You are very hard on yourself.

Kate nods slightly. She knows she mustn't laugh.

And you feel Ellen might help you with this?

Irving Mine is the art of sorrow.

Kate And Ellen's?

Irving The art of joy. Your sister is light and air and laughter. Your sister is hope. You understand, Mrs Lewis, I need your sister beside me. I can offer her forty pounds a week.

Ellen Forty?

Ellen tries not to show how impressed she is. The Maid returns.

Maid I'm sorry to interrupt, but Mr Irving is needed outside.

Kate Millie –

Maid His dog has soiled our carpet.

There is a moment's pause.

Ellen And what sort of omen is that?

3.

Music. As the setting changes, a dog, Charlie, runs across the stage, happily wagging its tail. Loveday, the stage manager, young, with a bright shock of hair, runs after. Edith comes on at the front.

Edith I've known many theatrical managers, and one characteristic united them all. Every single one was purse proud. Henry Irving was different. Generosity ran through his veins. He overpaid actors. 'Fat cats,' he said, 'hunt better than lean.'

The court at Elsinore comes flooding onto the stage, which becomes a romantic nineteenth-century castle, candlelit.

By the time the Lyceum was due to open on December thirtieth, 1878, he had an overdraft of twelve thousand pounds at the London and County Bank, which he had personally guaranteed.

Henry Irving was called many things, but nobody called him mean.

4.

The company stand around aimlessly. They've plainly been there for a long time. Gertrude and Claudius are both actors of a certain age, well used to the ups and downs of dress rehearsal. The year 1878 is projected.

Gertrude And is he coming back?

Loveday Of course he's coming back. He's gone to look for Ophelia.

Claudius He's going to get a shock when he sees her.

Loveday Why?

Claudius I'm saying nothing.

Gertrude Oh, do tell.

Claudius grins at Gertrude. Loveday turns to the company.

Loveday Mr Irving can't find Miss Terry, has anyone seen her?

Gertrude Not recently.

Claudius Have you tried wardrobe?

Gertrude Can you just let us know, does he intend to rehearse until dawn?

Claudius And beyond, knowing Henry.

Irving appears in tights and Elizabethan costume, all black, and with a blond wig.

Irving Has anyone seen Miss Terry?

Claudius She was in her dressing room at midnight. But that seems another age.

Irving What time is it now?

Loveday Gone three.

Irving shrugs, unperturbed.

I'm afraid you'll find, sir, that people are getting a little tired.

Irving I can't think why. We still have two acts to go.

Loveday Yes, I think that may be what's concerning them, sir.

Irving I hope everyone appreciates that I have cut forty per cent of the play.

Claudius Yes, and we still run five and a half hours.

Gertrude Can't we get on and kill Gertrude? I'm aching to go home.

Irving I carry the load and I'm fresh as a daisy. Let us find Miss Terry and resume.

Loveday Patience, please. Patience, everyone.

From the upstage entrance, Ellen appears. She is dressed head to toe in black. The movement stops and suddenly everyone is staring at her.

Ellen I believe you sent for me.

Irving I did.

Ellen Where exactly are we resuming?

Irving frowns.

Irving My intention was to make progress towards the mad scene, but I see you are not dressed for it.

Ellen I am dressed for it.

Irving As you are?

Ellen As I am.

Irving Are you sure?

Irving looks round, a little desperate.

I wanted to rehearse in costume.

Ellen I am in costume.

Irving It's a tradition that the mad scene should be played in white.

Ellen I'm playing it in black. With your permission, of course.

The whole company has fallen silent, watching the tennis match.

Irving I suggest we take a fifteen-minute break while I speak to Miss Terry. Loveday, please offer oysters and champagne to keep everyone going.

Loveday Sir, it's the middle of the night. Oysters may be hard to come by.

Irving I had ordered them in, anticipating disruption.

Loveday Sir.

Loveday turns to the company.

Oysters, everyone! Champagne!

Everyone goes chattering into the distance except Ellen and Irving.

Irving Very well, the mad scene.

Ellen Yes. My instinct is to do it in a way which is original.

Irving Yes.

Ellen I've studied the text and come to this conclusion. Ophelia must wear black. It's appropriate to her emotions. We can't do the plays in the same way every time.

Irving Indeed.

Ellen We have to waken the audience. We have to give them the unexpected.

Irving But not the unacceptable. Not shock for its own sake.

Irving nods, satisfied with how this is going.

Hamlet always works because it's a play. *Romeo and Juliet* never works because it's a poem.

Ellen nods, thinking this over.

Ellen You may be right, but if I can raise a query –

Irving Raise it.

Ellen About my own participation, about my role.

Irving Whatever you want.

Ellen Very well, if I may say: I have watched your rehearsals in astonishment. I do not believe that in the history of the British theatre there has ever been any manager with your attention to detail.

Irving Detail matters.

Ellen Indeed.

Irving Verbal. Visual. The articulation of the stage.

Ellen That too.

Irving Every actor must have intention, and they must be clothed and surrounded in a way which supports that intention. At every moment.

Ellen I would say in all these areas – I do not mean to embarrass you – but you are at a level of your own. I have never seen any production of any play anywhere so fully prepared and completely realised as under your supervision.

Irving is taken aback.

Irving Thank you.

Ellen Nobody can fault you for diligence.

Irving It's in my character.

Ellen However I have noticed that your attention to detail does not seem to extend to the women in the company.

Irving Ah.

Ellen Perhaps I am mistaken, but it seems that in this company the women are left to do as they please.

Irving is careful.

Irving You feel that, do you?

Ellen You seem to prioritise the men.

Irving The males?

Ellen Throughout the rehearsals, I've tried to gain your attention.

Irving You have it always.

Ellen When I've performed a scene, I've sought your response. I've looked for guidance. Ophelia is not an easy part. I am alone. I've been left alone. I am not sure why.

Irving doesn't seem to want to speak.

Occasionally in the past in other companies I've been characterised as too talkative –

Irving Surely not?

Ellen Too spontaneous –

Irving I don't feel that –

Ellen Too ready to spill with whatever random thought is passing through my head –

Irving I welcome that –

Ellen I have a brain like a bird's nest, it's all bits of straw –

Irving Hardly –

Ellen I'm uneducated, I'm undisciplined. One actor told me I change like the weather. One moment, he said, in the grip of an obsession, next it's forgotten, he said it was like acting with fog –

Irving Hardly –

Ellen But on this occasion, I feel I am constructing my performance on my own. You say nothing, Henry. Do I displease you?

Again, he doesn't speak.

I fear I shall fail as Ophelia. I fear I shall fail very badly. I am haunted by this fear day and night. There are times when I cannot sleep. I cannot sit still. Edy and Teddy say I am lately distraught. At breakfast I put sugar on my bread and marmalade in my tea. And I look to you to help dispel this fear with words of reassurance. And when I look, there is nothing. Just silence. For goodness' sake, the reason I have not discussed wearing black with you is because I have not discussed anything with you.

Irving No.

Ellen Even Gertrude is occasionally thrown a scrap. I am thrown nothing. What is my offence?

She waits.

Irving No offence.

Ellen Really?

Irving None.

Ellen Why then are you not speaking to me?

Irving shakes his head, embarrassed.

Irving You drag this from me. I would not say this if I were not at the point of a gun.

Ellen And about to fire.

Irving shrugs.

Irving I am uncomfortable with women.

Ellen As a man?

Irving Women embarrass me.

Ellen Ah. Generally?

Irving Yes.

Ellen All women?

Irving Most. From childhood. Men are comforting to me. Women make me feel – I don't know –

Ellen Nervous?

Irving Unsettled. But more than that –

Ellen There's more?

Irving hesitates, then is suddenly decisive.

Irving Ellen, listen: I do not speak to you because you are perfect.

Ellen Perfect?

Irving Yes.

Ellen That's impossible.

Irving There is nothing to say.

Ellen But I vary my performance at each rehearsal.

Irving You do.

Ellen And so?

Irving I wait eagerly to see what you will do next. It's always different.

Ellen Then how can it always be perfect?

Irving One of the mysteries of theatre, my dear.

Ellen stands, stunned.

Ellen Is that really what you think?

Irving If you want me to give you specific directives, then I have only one.

Ellen Please.

Irving I don't wish to be overbearing.

Ellen On the contrary. To me, at least, you are under-bearing.

Irving Very well then. Surely in *Hamlet* only Hamlet wears black.

There is a moment.

I wear black.

Ellen I see.

Irving Naturally, if you *want* to wear black –

Ellen No, no, forgive me – I thought only of myself. Typical. All too typical, it had not occurred to me –

Irving Perhaps I am old-fashioned, but generally, in the play *Hamlet*, the role of Hamlet is taken to be the leading role –

Ellen Of course. I agree. Who wouldn't?

Irving And for that reason probably black costumes should not be scattered promiscuously throughout the cast.

Irving looks mortified. Ellen is flustered.

I know this may sound brutal, but Hamlet needs to stand out.

Ellen Understood.

Irving You may think me overly theatrical –

Ellen Not at all –

Irving I've been accused of it –

Ellen Not in the slightest. And by the way I've never understood why 'theatrical' should be a term of abuse –

Irving Nor me –

Ellen Nobody says of music that it's too musical, why then do they say of theatre that it's too theatrical?

Irving I really don't know. Though you yourself have a naturalness I envy –

Ellen Is naturalness really such a good thing? Is Hamlet natural? He speaks in verse for a start, which very few people do.

But Irving is persisting, each more courteous and deferential than the other.

Irving No, no, but I noticed last time –

Ellen You mean the Garrick play?

Irving Sometimes acting beside you I seem stiff and awkward.

Ellen nods slightly, hesitates.

Ellen If I may say –

Irving Anything –

Ellen I don't want to interfere –

Irving Interfere!

Ellen I have no status. But I observed the last time I acted with you, you come down from your dressing room –

Irving I do –

Ellen Always leaving plenty of time –

Irving I try to –

Ellen You stand in the wings for several minutes, ready to make your entrance –

She stops.

Irving Well?

Ellen Is it possible you over-prepare?

Irving Goodness.

Ellen Don't the minutes you spend before entering make you overly tense, too wound up, too full of nerves? Rather than making you ready, do they not make you clumsy?

Irving has begun to pace, as though a door is being unlocked.

Irving I have never thought such a thing –

Ellen Do those moments of delay not have the effect of making you stilted and self-conscious?

Irving Well –

Ellen Myself, I never leave my dressing room till the last possible moment. I put down the newspaper I am reading, or the light novel, I fly down the stairs, sometimes I confess

I even take the banisters, and then at the last possible moment –

She makes a gesture as of a ghost passing through a room.

I pass. I pass from one world to another. I cross the invisible line between the real world and the imagined. There is no passport, there are no border guards. There is no change of language, nor of morals and manners. I am abroad, but I am at home. I am the same person who a moment ago was reading the novel unobserved. And now of the fact that a thousand people are observing me – closely – I am genuinely unaware.

Irving nods, grave.

Irving You may be right. That may be my error.

Ellen I would bet folding money on it.

Irving I shall try to be more last-minute. It's a good tip.

Ellen It's not a tip. It's an attitude.

She has said this more sharply than she intended.

Irving Yes. You're right.

Ellen And also –

Irving Yes?

Ellen Now I'm sounding a scold –

Irving Not at all –

Ellen Occasionally – this is just an idea –

Irving No please –

Ellen I don't mean to overburden you –

Irving We have a couple of minutes before the troupe returns –

Ellen I have a feeling that your acting could be improved if from time to time you directed your gaze at the other actor.

Irving is more defensive.

Irving Do I not do that?

Ellen As I said, playing Ophelia can be a lonely business – it's not fun to drown yourself – and it would be less lonely if I was looked at. If I was seen.

Irving nods, grave. It's hard to know how he's taking it.

You have a brooding intensity which is exciting, and in my own view that intensity would not be compromised by contact with other members of the company. It would be enhanced.

Irving Thank you. I shall look out for that.

Ellen It's just an idea.

Irving Look at the other actors, you say?

Ellen shrugs slightly.

Ellen It's always worked for me.

Irving That's interesting. Always remembering, mind you, that Shakespeare's heroes are isolated figures, they live in their minds.

Ellen Yes. But they also live in the world.

Irving nods, taking this in.

Irving This has been an unexpected interlude.

Ellen A good one, I hope.

Irving I sent the company away with the intention of giving you instruction. But instead I have learnt from you. We must do this again.

The two of them stand for a moment, looking at each other.

Ellen I went to the madhouse.

Irving Pardon me?

Ellen I didn't tell you. I made a visit. To observe the lunatics.

Irving In the madhouse?

Ellen Yes.

Irving Alone?

Ellen I observed them for several days. I wanted to enrich my performance as Ophelia. I wanted to ensure my mannerisms were authentic.

Irving And did you?

Ellen smiles.

Ellen To be honest, no. I watched them. But I found them overly theatrical. It was if they were playing mad. Nobody would have believed them.

And now they both smile. Then there is the noise of the chattering company returning.

Claudius I simply do not understand how any human being can defile oysters with lemon juice.

Gertrude I shall eat oysters how I wish.

Claudius Henry, am I not right? Back me up. Support me.

Irving Hmm?

Claudius This woman douses oysters in lemon juice. And in our play, you ask me to pretend to be in love with her!

Gertrude Then pretend! Pretend!

Much mocking laughter from everyone. They are all cheerfully going back to their old positions, but Irving is transfixed by Ellen, the two of them unmoving.

Loveday All right, please stand by. Stand by. Mr Irving, Miss Terry.

The other actors go to the side, as Irving and Ellen take centre stage.

Ellen Mr Irving, do you wish me to change?

Irving Not if it will take time, no. Wear black for now. But only for now.

And without pause he goes straight into the scene.

'I loved you not.'

Ellen 'I was the more deceived.'

Irving 'Get thee to a nunnery. Why wouldst thou be a breeder of sinners?'

Ellen 'O help him, you sweet heavens!'

Irving 'If thou dost marry, I'll give thee this plague for thy dowry: be thou as chaste as ice, as pure as snow, thou shalt not escape calumny. Get thee to a nunnery: go, farewell. Or if thou wilt needs marry, marry a fool, for wise men know well enough what monsters you make of them. To a nunnery, go and quickly too. Farewell. Go to. I'll no more on't. It hath made me mad. I say, we will have no more marriages. Those that are married already, all but one shall live. The rest shall keep as they are. To a nunnery, go.'

Irving stalks off. Ellen is left alone.

Ellen 'O what a noble mind is here o'erthrown!'

Edith appears, carrying timber.

5.

Edith As soon as I could, I started work in the costume shop of Henry Irving's theatre. And I'm proud to say I made costumes for my mother. But then thirty years later, well into the twentieth century, when Ellen was much older, I had the idea of building a theatre in the garden of her house at Smallhythe. People said, why on earth would anyone build a theatre in Kent? I said, if the work's good enough, the audience will come.

6.

Hamlet *rehearsals have been replaced by an empty floor in Smallhythe. Tony Atwood (born Clare, aka The Brat), fifties, is small, exquisite, in men's clothes. She is sweeping the floor of the barn. The year 1922 is projected. Edith turns.*

Edith I don't see why I end up having to do all this myself. For goodness' sake, where are you, Chris?

She calls offstage to an unseen companion.

Come on, you're far stronger than me.

Tony Is there more?

Edith We've scarcely started.

Christabel aka Christopher St John, aka Master Baby, arrives carrying planks over her shoulder. She is a startling woman, in her fifties, dressed as a man and bulging out of her corduroy trousers.

Chris Timber!

Tony I can't believe it. How many trees are going to have to die?

Chris A forest. Of English oak. And then some.

Chris has put hers down.

Edith We need to get this done as fast as possible. We need to get this theatre up before my mother even notices.

Tony We're building a theatre in her garden. You think Ellen won't notice?

Chris She'll notice.

Tony She's always been against.

Chris She says she comes here to escape the theatre, not to have it pursue her.

Edith She's going to love it when she sees it.

Chris Are you sure? You've always underestimated Ellen Terry.

Tony Why don't we stop for tea?

Edith I've never underestimated her. On the contrary. I tell you, Teddy and I once stumbled on a rare point of agreement. A child of Ellen Terry has only two choices: surrender or fight. Defiance has been my only means of survival.

Tony Well, I'm in favour of a theatre. I admire the heroic and the hopeless.

Edith The Brat's in favour of everything. And everyone. That's why the boy's such darling company.

Tony Thank you.

Edith kisses her.

Edith And so good at stopping spiteful arguments, which used to arise, Christopher, between you and me. With our naturally contrary personalities.

Chris I don't know what you're talking about.

Edith You know bloody well. We did nothing but squabble before Tony arrived.

Tony I love being referee.

Tony has put her broom aside to pour tea on a table at the side. Edith goes to join her.

Edith I don't care if my mother approves or not. We are building the Barn according to first principles. Nail by nail. Our theatre will have no class divisions. Everyone will pay the same price and have the same view. No balcony for the plebs, no stalls for the rich. An open stage, back to the Elizabethan model – no fourth wall. We speak direct because what we have to say is important.

Edith is firm.

Whatever else, we must be sure that the seats are not too comfortable.

Chris Comfortable seats are the death of the drama.

Tony No cushions?

Chris Certainly not.

Edith The things the Pioneers have to say are far too urgent.

Chris We're not in this game to please people.

Tony Then I fear we can safely predict success. Come on, drink tea.

They all smile as Chris stops shifting planks and comes over to join them. The three women, all dressed as men, stand looking out over the lawn.

Edith You know she's actually going to be here.

Tony Who?

Edith My mother. This weekend. She's exhausted. We need to take care of her.

Tony Put her to bed and I'll bring her hot lemon and ginger.

Chris Excellent. If Ellen's here, I can make some serious progress on her memoirs.

Edith I'm not sure, Master Baby.

Tony Honestly, I think you should allow her some quiet.

Chris Why?

Edith Does it really make her happy? Raking over the past?

Chris That's what a memoir is, Matka.

Edith thinks a moment. Chris drinks her tea.

Edith Twenty-five years with Irving, together on the stage. Twenty-seven plays. And at the end, what does she have left? Every weekend you lead her back to the nineteenth century. It disturbs her.

Chris If anyone has a problem with the past, it's simple. Get it down on paper. Writing your memoirs is like emptying your bowels. It's hygienic. You feel better afterwards.

Tony I'm sure we shall all treasure that image, Chris.

Chris scoffs, intolerant.

Chris Why are you so certain that our biographical sessions depress her? It's a feminist tale. Victorian England, supposedly so strict, so straitlaced, and yet a mother with two bastard children is its most beloved citizen. Explain that.

Edith I wish it were as simple as you make out.

Chris How do you see it then?

Edith The strong woman loses the only man she ever loved.

Chris You think that's the secret, do you? You think that's the key? I'll write that down if you like. Put it on the frigging flyleaf. 'Ellen Terry: Lost the man she loved.'

But Edith ignores her sarcasm.

Edith What's wrong with that? It's the truth. You're her biographer. A child-bride was married before she knew anything – at the age of sixteen, married to a man of forty-seven –

Chris George Watts –

Edith Yes. For ten sexless months only. And then what happens next? She has two illegitimate children with the man she does love –

Chris Are you talking about your father?

Edith I certainly am. William Godwin lives with Ellen but refuses to divorce his wife. A few years later, he abandons her. Ellen lives in utter squalor and wretchedness with two babies and absolutely no hope for the future. Later, he dies. Imagine. Imagine the effect of that.

Edith shakes her head, upset.

Irving comes to save her. And what do they call this woman when she first arrives? The scarlet woman of the Lyceum. The wench. The serpent. The facts speak for themselves.

Chris If those are the facts.

Edith I don't see how you can dispute them.

Chris I can't dispute the facts, but I can dispute the interpretation.

Edith Can you indeed?

Edith looks at her uncharitably.

Chris For a start, in all our conversations, Ellen has never once mentioned her great love for your father.

Edith Of course not.

Chris Why should that be?

Edith Because the soul of her acting is concealment.

Chris And you think she also conceals in life?

Edith Please! My mother?

Edith laughs at how obvious it is.

Chris Does it never occur to you, Matka, when you bring up Ellen's obsession with Godwin, what you're talking about is not Ellen, but yourself?

Edith I don't think so.

Chris Well I do. I've lived with you, remember?

Edith I'm not likely to forget.

Chris And I can say that being abandoned by your father at the age of five is something you've never got over.

Edith Oh, is that right? Hark, the Kentish psychiatrist!

Chris If you're talking about facts, then that's a fact. Your father didn't love you. And he certainly didn't love Teddy. Your father didn't want your brother, and he didn't want you. Finally. And that's what made you both what you are.

Edith I'm going to excuse that remark on the grounds that taking it seriously would lead us into another flaming row.

Tony Boys, boys, a little rural quiet, please.

There is an uneasy truce.

Sylvia Pankhurst's new pamphlet has arrived. It's in the sitting room when you take a break from your labours.

Chris Pankhurst can't teach us anything.

Edith She can try.

Chris Talk, talk, talk and all to no frigging effect. Who cares?

Tony We care.

Edith And to be fair, whatever you think of them, the suffragettes have exploded the odd bomb.

Tony Who else ever blew up the Glasgow aqueduct?

Chris Oh come on, even I set fire to a post-box. Fat lot of good it did.

Edith is suddenly firm.

Edith We need to be clear: why are we building this theatre?

Tony To annoy your mother?

Edith No, Tony. We are building it to change the world. The Pioneer Players will take contemporary subjects and confront the audience with their own ignorance and prejudice. Plays about suffrage. Plays about women.

Tony To an audience of thirty, four drunks and a dog from Romney Marsh.

Edith That's how we'll start, yes. And at the end, we'll achieve something far more effective than anything Sylvia Pankhurst ever writes. She wants their minds. I want their souls.

Edith smiles and turns at Chris.

Can you manage more planks?

Chris Willingly.

Tony It's steak and kidney for supper.

Chris Marvellous.

Tony And local ale.

Chris Perfect. A perfect day. Shifting timber. Is there anything better than getting things done?

Chris goes out, reanimated. Tony resumes sweeping, Edith drinks her tea, a gentleness between them.

Edith I don't know what I'd do without you, Tony. Chris and I did nothing but fight till you came.

Tony I've always believed in the power of three. It works.

Edith It works when the third is you.

They work a few moments, in accord.

Tony Are you worried about your mother?

Edith Always.

Tony She's always cheerful.

Edith No. She always seems cheerful. Her cheerfulness covers a melancholy which could one day overwhelm her.

Tony You think her cheerfulness is false?

Edith It's not false. It's willed. That's different.

Tony You think she puts it on?

Edith For my mother, appearing cheerful is simply a form of good manners. To give in to melancholy is to risk infecting others. Why burden other people? That's what she thinks.

There is a moment as they work.

Underneath, Ellen has nothing but regret.

Tony Why?

Edith It's been a life on the stage.

Tony Then why are you building one?

Edith Me?

Tony Yes. Why are you building a stage?

Edith turns away, working quietly.

Edith I told you. I want change. I don't know how else to get it.

7.

The two women go on sweeping as Teddy arrives quietly to address us.

Teddy Myself, I dreamt of a theatre without actors. I became insanely excited when I read Eleonora Duse. 'To save the Theatre, the Theatre must be destroyed. The actors and actresses must all die of the plague. They make theatre impossible.'

The women go, and are replaced by the dressing rooms of the Lyceum Theatre.

The only kind of revolution which interests me is total revolution. What Christ wanted, in fact, if you bother to read him properly. A total overturning.

8.

The year 1880 is projected. Irving is asleep by the fire in his dressing room. Ellen in an elegant dressing gown comes in, carrying candles. She looks for a moment and he wakes. His dog, Charlie, is asleep beside him.

Ellen I've woken you.

Irving No. I shouldn't have been asleep.

He smiles and nods.

Come in, there's some good port that I put aside for us.

Ellen Are you becoming too fond of drink?

Irving I'm an actor.

He nods at a bottle of port on a tray for her to pour.

And criticism sends me to sleep.

Ellen Who's been criticising?

Irving The daily press.

He waves a newspaper he had discarded.

Ellen Oh for goodness' sake –

Irving This one says I'm a pig who's been taught to be play the fiddle –

Ellen You must admit that's quite funny –

Irving And tell me if it's true –

Ellen Is what true?

Irving That I say 'Gud'?

Ellen Sometimes.

Irving Instead of 'God'?

Ellen People come from miles to hear you say 'Gud'. 'I pray to Gud!'

Irving And do I drag my leg?

Ellen Oh please, Henry, you should ignore it.

Irving But do I?

Ellen You have a heavy leg. Yes.

Irving It drags?

Ellen Why do you read it?

Irving Because I'm not just an actor. I'm a manager. Livelihoods depend on me.

She hands him a glass of port.

Why is someone so unsuited to tights choosing to spend his whole life in tights? It's strange. I can't walk, I can't talk, and I have no face to speak of.

Ellen Otherwise you have all the equipment.

Irving As you say.

Ellen And while we're on the subject, let's face it, you say 'Cut-thrut dug'.

Irving When do I say it?

Ellen You said it tonight.

Irving In *The Merchant*?

Ellen Certainly. For 'cut-throat dog'.

Ellen imitates him, brilliantly.

'You call me misbeliever, cut-thrut dug,
And spit upon my Jewish gaberdine . . .'

Irving It can't be as bad as that.

Ellen It's as bad as that. And when you're playing Mathias in *The Bells*: 'Tack this rup frum mey neck . . .'

Irving All right, very humorous, very funny –

Ellen I'm just telling you how you speak –

Irving How do I speak?

Ellen With thick 'r's and a lot of rubato.

Irving People like my rubato. They revel in it.

Ellen When they can understand it.

Irving The sound and the sense are one. Surely you know that?

Irving waves the newspaper at her.

And by the way, the papers don't care much for you either.

Ellen Why not?

Irving Oh the usual. They say you speak too fast.

Ellen They always say that. The only time the English admire speed is at the Derby.

Irving They say Portia shouldn't flirt.

Ellen I don't flirt.

Irving They say it's not an erotic part.

Ellen It is when I play it.

Irving Exactly. That's their objection. 'She's a lawyer,' they say. 'How can she be sexual?' Remember Henry James?

Ellen He hates the theatre. Too much hugging and kissing, he says.

Irving 'Ellen Terry is too sexual to be a great actress.'

Ellen For Henry James, a handshake is too sexual. A shared pot of tea is dangerously licentious. What's wrong with the man? Does he think I will leap from the stage and seduce him?

Irving In his nightmares, yes.

Ellen An affair with me would straighten out his prose.

They both smile. Ellen stands behind him, very close.

You're not going home tonight.

Irving Are you asking or guessing?

Ellen Guessing.

Irving On what basis?

Ellen Precedent.

Irving You're right. I shall sleep at the Garrick Club.

Ellen You sleep at the club quite often.

Irving You keep track of my nights?

Ellen Only because you keep track of mine.

Irving You're my leading lady. I need to look after you. I need to know you're content.

Ellen reaches down and kisses him.

Ellen I'm content.

There is a moment, then she moves to the chair opposite him.

The hour after the show is my favourite hour of the day. I like empty theatres.

Irving Me too.

Ellen This time together is precious.

Irving looks at her a moment, hesitating.

Irving I hope I won't spoil it by mentioning the problem of your son.

Ellen Teddy?

Irving Yes.

Ellen Teddy's a problem?

Irving You must have noticed. Edward is disliked.

Ellen By whom?

Irving By more or less everyone. He is not a popular figure.

Ellen And is that because he's my son?

Irving No.

Irving shifts, uneasy.

Did you know that the other spear carriers threw him from the battlements of Elsinore? The supernumeraries jostle him continually. There is backstage violence. They mean him harm.

Ellen He didn't tell me.

Irving And they're a tough bunch.

Ellen I've noticed.

Irving Muscled to a man.

Ellen nods gravely.

I took your son in because I thought him promising. He can act. In a strange sort of way. But the happiness of my ensemble is paramount.

Ellen doesn't want to concede.

Ellen, theatre is a group activity.

Ellen Are you saying he doesn't fit in?

Irving Edward is your son, so if you instruct me to defend him, then I shall do my best. I await your instructions.

Ellen Have you been thinking of putting him out on the street?

Irving doesn't answer.

Teddy is an unusual character. He's finding his feet.

Irving Until he finds them, he would be wise to shut his mouth. He appears incapable of being silent.

Ellen He has always found it hard.

Irving From his lips flows a stream of pretentious nonsense which tests everyone's nerves to the limit.

Ellen He's adolescent.

Irving Even so. 'A theatre of pure movement and design!'

Ellen I've heard.

Irving 'A place only of sound and light and vision!' 'Pure space.' 'Pure spirit.' 'A theatre without text!'

Ellen Is it possible that my son is an artistic visionary?

Irving Is it possible that your son is a jackass?

Irving has spoken with real vehemence. Ellen is, for the first time aback.

Worse, he disparages the work.

Ellen Not openly?

Irving Yes. Openly.

Ellen That's foolish.

Irving Foolish? It's incendiary. He wanders backstage telling other actors that the Lyceum style is long dead.

Ellen Are you saying he's rude about you?

Irving Never.

Ellen When it was you who took him in?

Irving He's not that stupid.

Ellen May I ask this question?

Irving Ask anything.

Ellen Is he rude about me?

Irving has to smile at her vulnerability.

Irving Rest easy. You and I are spared.

Ellen Thank God for that.

Irving Only you and I approach his high standards. Apparently, we are consummate practitioners.

Ellen Of what exactly?

Irving Well, there you have it. Of a faded and musty technique which was outdated before he was born.

Ellen Oh, really!

Irving He loves me because I'm powerful.

Ellen What sort of reason is that?

Irving I'm a dictator. He admires dictators. He believes the theatre, like the realm, should be dominated by one man. That's me. So I am forgiven. He sits with his fellow actors and tells them he dreams of a theatre without actors. And then he's surprised when they propel him from the scenery.

Ellen frowns, disturbed.

Ellen Surely they don't take him seriously? It's obvious. He's a child.

Irving You must know: there's a tone.

Ellen What tone is that?

Irving The tone used by people who consider themselves artistically advanced. They manage at once to be both whining and arrogant. Self-pity is combined with utter self-certainty.

Ellen Then why do people take any notice?

Irving Why do you think?

Ellen *Why?*

Irving Because they hate the hypocrisy! So do I!

Irving has raised his voice, provoked himself.

Edward draws his wages here at the stage door – he draws them willingly – he eats and drinks as much as he likes –

Ellen I know –

Irving Ellen, I am not an ungenerous soul –

Ellen On the contrary –

Irving And I don't hold grudges. But here is a young man who has no scruples about living well at my expense.

Ellen I know.

Irving I sound selfish.

Ellen No.

Irving At dinner he sits next to his mother at the head of the table. All favours are given him, all privileges.

Ellen He benefits from your kindness, Henry. Always.

Irving He has fought for nothing, and he wants for nothing.

Ellen I agree.

Irving He's introduced to the politicians, the judges, the artists, the writers who flock to this theatre –

Ellen He values the encounters –

Irving Who wouldn't? The most substantial people in London come to the Lyceum. At last the drama in England has status. It is *the* supreme art form.

Ellen Thanks to you –

Irving And your son, who has the good fortune to be set down in the middle of the whole damned bagwash, is twenty years old. So what conclusion does he draw? Everything which currently occurs on the British stage is without value. It's all spit and frippery. And the only art which is any good is the art which exists in Gordon Craig's imagination.

Ellen Yes. It's true. He does think that.

Irving And what provokes the company most, his gift for unrealised fantasy brings him amazing success with women.

Ellen Really?

Irving You must have noticed.

Ellen You don't notice. Not when it's your son.

Irving Men who talk of achieving things are always far more compelling than men who actually achieve them.

Ellen Is that right?

Irving But sorry – success with women can also create resentment.

Irving is suddenly steel.

Ellen, I need a happy company. When my company's unhappy, so am I.

Ellen nods and gets up to pour him more port. She's gentle.

Ellen What are you saying? Are you blaming me? People tell me I spoiled him. He was told he was a genius because he could write and draw. Thousands of children can write and draw.

Irving Then why did you use that word?

Ellen He was born out of wedlock. I was worried for him.

There is a moment's silence.

His father was an architect, a designer, a painter, I believe of the first rank.

Irving You loved him? Godwin, I mean?

Ellen nods, unable to answer.

Ellen I loved him so much I had to make myself a promise.

Irving What promise?

Ellen Never to fall in love again. It's too painful.

Irving sits contemplating her. Then he reaches out his hand to her. She takes it. They sit a moment.

Irving But Edward has a sister –

Ellen Yes –

Irving Edy works in our costume shop –

Ellen Yes –

Irving Also illegitimate –

Ellen Yes –

Irving She's faultlessly loyal.

Ellen I spoiled Teddy because he reminded me of Godwin. I barely noticed Edy because she reminded me of me.

Irving She seems not to have suffered.

Ellen Edy? Not suffered? Perhaps.

Ellen smiles to herself, not convinced. Then she lets go his hand and gets up, restless.

Henry, do you never worry we're becoming too settled?

Irving Who?

Ellen You and me. Your theatre. Are we too set in our ways?

Irving What makes you say that?

Ellen Historical pageants, do you never tire of them?

Irving Never.

Ellen Are we listening to what Teddy is actually saying? The boy may have something to tell us.

Irving looks at her a moment.

Irving My life is the Lyceum, Ellen. I wake and I pay the bills from my bed. In my bath I plan the repertory. As I eat my eggs, I read the accounts. I am in the building by ten and I leave past midnight. Every day of the season. A candle is spluttering in the foyer – I am immediately informed. I find the person to deal with it. On Thursday last, in Row S, a rip was found in the material covering one of the seats. S24. The house manager was indisposed. An hour before the performance I was on my knees with needle and thread. I then played Othello immediately afterwards. If not me, who?

Ellen I understand.

Irving gets up and moves across the room.

Irving I am my work. What else am I? If you want your son to continue in the company, please tell him: I have sacrificed everything. He has sacrificed nothing.

Ellen Why is it sacrifice if it's what you want to do?

Irving looks at her, not answering.

Henry, you don't think dreaming is part of life?

Irving Part, yes. But only part.

Irving smiles.

Did you know that in Shakespeare there are seventeen 'no's to every one 'yes'?

Ellen I didn't know that.

Irving Someone did a count.

Ellen I'm astonished.

Irving All his power is in the negative.

He looks at her gravely.

One day I too will have to say no.

9.

The Lyceum goes. Music. Way upstage, a vision, Isadora Duncan, aged twenty-six, dances by in shafts of abstract light. She is wearing what seem like rags. As she passes through, she launches herself into the air, in connection with the music. Teddy, thirty-two, watches from the side, then moves to a table in a dressing room to start drawing.

10.

Another dressing room. Berlin. The date is projected: 1904. Teddy is working with a pencil as Isadora comes in fresh from the stage. She is American.

Isadora Did you miss me entirely?

Teddy No. I was watching.

Isadora I didn't see you.

Teddy I was standing at the side. You were wonderful, as always.

Isadora Would you like some champagne?

Teddy I don't need champagne.

Isadora But you'll have some?

Isadora goes to open a bottle.

Teddy I went back to work straight away. I'm disturbed at the prospect of moving again. Everyone wants to see Isadora Duncan.

Isadora But you're not unhappy?

Teddy Every day I wake up and I'm not in England. I miss my mother, of course I do, but nothing else.

She leans over and kisses him on the top of his head.

And meanwhile I have to design my *King Lear*.

Isadora How are the designs?

Teddy Promising. High walls. Shadows. No clutter. Humans scurrying in the dark below.

Teddy shrugs.

It's early days.

Isadora You know full well it'll never happen. You'll find some excuse. I know you already. 'Rehearsals are too short.' 'The theatre's too cramped.' 'No one understands my vision.'

Teddy When I left London, I made the decision. No more mediocrity. Only perfection. Why else do you think I'm living with you? The first perfect thing I had ever seen.

Isadora Are you speaking artistically?

Teddy Artistically. Emotionally. Both.

He gets up and kisses her, then goes back to his chair.

You alone appreciate that theatre is movement. It's shape and action and colour and light –

Isadora Since I was a little girl –

Teddy It's a temple. What else? It takes us back to the gods.

Isadora They kept teaching me steps. I used to say: what use are steps?

Teddy Steps are as bad as words. The theatre died when it became a prisoner of words.

Isadora It's sensation we need, Teddy. Not meaning.

He smiles at her.

Teddy Even so, I still wish we didn't have to go to Vienna.

Isadora We're only going for a day.

Teddy Exactly. I'm longing for France. The South. The sun.

Isadora If I don't dance, we don't make money.

Teddy If we serve the gods, the gods will look after us.

Isadora drinks her champagne and sits opposite him. He carries on drawing.

Isadora I can't believe how penniless you are.

Teddy Why? Why does it surprise you?

Isadora Because you're so famous.

Teddy Famous, yes. Employed, no.

Isadora You could change that in a moment if you so wanted. How do you learn except by doing things?

Teddy looks at her a moment.

Teddy I can do the job. Yes. I can do the job as well as anyone else. But the world is full of people who can do the job. I was an actor, and not a bad actor. But I used to watch Henry Irving and my mother from the wings, and I knew I was wasting my time. They were perfection. They were unimprovable. Oh, I was fine in repertory. Everyone's fine in repertory. Today this, tomorrow that. Pointless dressing up and grimacing. Representing reality! And for what? It's a losing battle. Reality always wins. Isn't reality so much richer than its representation? How can we win that game? Let's fight on ground we can take. And every time I pointed out the ridiculousness of it all, the thugs in Irving's company set upon me. Bodily. No, really. So one day I picked up a pencil and began to draw. And the power which had eluded me as an actor flowed through my hand. It flowed, and it flows as your dancing flows.

Teddy smiles, perfectly content.

What you do in dance is what I aim to do in theatre. You leave the audience to decide what it means. No words. No slogans. No homilies. No actors moving like trams along predestinate lines, their brows sweating with the fear of forgetting what they've been ordered to say. No axiomatic little stories with a moral. God, how I hate morals.

Isadora You do.

Teddy When I watch you, I see the thing itself. Pure.

He raises his glass of champagne.

That's why I love you so much.

Isadora You love me?

Teddy Yes. I've told you.

Isadora Have you told your wife?

Teddy Have I told her?

Isadora Have you told her what's happened? Does she even know where you are?

Teddy My wife would understand. She wants my happiness, just as I want hers.

Isadora But you haven't told her?

Teddy makes a gesture of hopelessness.

Do you write to her at all?

Teddy I told you. I'm not good with words. Elena and I don't have a neurotic relationship. We don't fuss.

Isadora gets up, unamused.

People are like plays, you can't go on loving the same one. For goodness' sake, she knows who I am.

Isadora is silent. Teddy is annoyed.

Why are you taking her part? You don't even know her.

Isadora I'm not taking her part. I'm taking my own. Because I know you will one day do the same thing to me.

Teddy Ridiculous!

Isadora Is it? You don't think you'll betray me?

Teddy Why would I betray you?

Isadora For the same reason you're now betraying your wife.

Isadora looks at him a moment.

I know we're both free and I'm happy with it. It's what I've always wanted and now here it is. But I admit I'm scared.

Teddy Scared?

Isadora No, really. Both you and I attract ridicule. Perhaps that's why we're drawn to each other. The other night a man shouted out, 'You're a fraud!' Yes. And the rest of the audience stayed silent. Nobody dissented. Another time, someone said loudly, 'She dances like a giraffe.' And people laughed. I say this only to you, I hear these voices, I hear them all the time.

Teddy We all hear these voices. The rat at the back of the head.

Isadora Your rats may be in your head, but mine are in the audience.

Teddy shakes his head, annoyed.

Teddy Why do you think I had to leave England? They're ruled by fear. Fear of being thought pretentious.

The put-down. The sneer. The mockery. It's all the English are good for. I became indifferent to ridicule.

Isadora And yet you left?

Teddy Yes. I left.

Isadora So you can't have been wholly indifferent?

She looks at him a moment.

It must have hurt? However well you disguise it.

For once he doesn't want to answer. She is moved by his sudden vulnerability.

What does your mother think?

Teddy Of what?

Isadora Of you, Teddy? What does Ellen think?

Teddy Ellen? I've never dared ask.

Isadora Why not?

Teddy It's too important. It would mean too much.

11.

Edith appears quietly at the side of the stage.

Edith My brother had at least thirteen children by the end of his life. With many different women.
   I had no children. At any point. With anyone.
   It would be hard to say which of us disliked children more.

The Berlin dressing room disappears. Irving crosses the stage as Malvolio, cross-gartered, in yellow stockings.

Irving 'I'll be revenged on the whole pack of you.'

The entire Irving company assembles, singing the final lines of Twelfth Night.

Company 'A great while ago the world begun
  With hey, ho, the wind and the rain,
  But that's all one, our play is done,
  And we'll strive to please you every day.'

12.

A swagged curtain descends on the company to tumultuous applause. It rises again to a full-scale standing ovation. The date 1883 is projected. Irving stands exhausted at the centre. He endures the applause, rather than accepts it. Ellen is more gracious. Wave after wave of applause and cheering – Irving lifting his arm to say thank you, then turning to his company for a last bow. The curtain finally comes down. He calls up into the flies.

Irving No more, please. No more. We can't do any more. It must be enough. Enthusiasm must have its limits. Hold the curtain please!

They begin to walk backstage as the scenery is cleared around them. Loveday shouts to everyone as they leave.

Loveday That's Boston, that's Boston everyone! St Louis tomorrow. All meet at the train at nine o'clock. Don't be late. And there's a supper in City Hall for anyone who wants it.

The company starts to wander off, chattering excitedly at the end of a hard evening's work. Laughter, good humour. Ellen, dressed as Viola, lingers a moment.

Irving It's better, surely you must admit, it's better. They loved it.

Ellen They don't love *Twelfth Night*. They love us. It's different.

Loveday has come over to talk to Irving.

Loveday There's a crowd already at your dressing room, sir.

Irving Thank you.

Loveday The Mayor of Boston is expecting you.

Irving Tell him I'm on my way.

Loveday Sir.

Loveday goes. Ellen and Irving are left alone on the huge stage, a few stagehands going by in the distance.

Irving The Americans always wanted to like us, and I was determined to give them every opportunity to do so. You hear them at the end?

Ellen Yes.

Irving What an ovation! Have you ever heard such a noise?

Irving looks at her mistrustfully.

Something tells me you still don't admire my Malvolio.

Ellen I've said before.

Irving You mean you liked it no better tonight?

Irving waits. Ellen doesn't answer.

I'm trying to please you, Ellen. I'm trying to win your approval.

Ellen You're trying too hard.

Irving Still?

Ellen He's too angry. It isn't funny. They're scared of you.

Irving Malvolio is humiliated. I see his fate as tragic.

Ellen You see everything as tragic. *Twelfth Night* is meant to be a comedy.

Irving has detected her tone.

Irving Something is wrong. Tell me what's bothering you.

Ellen Nothing.

Irving You're happy in America?

Ellen I miss my children, of course. We've been here six months.

Irving No English company has ever been here so long.

Ellen No.

Irving Or been so admired.

Ellen No.

Irving What then?

Ellen I hesitate to say.

Irving waits.

At Niagara Falls –

Irving Yes –

Ellen I wanted to throw myself in.

Irving Why did you want that?

Irving is taken aback. Ellen shrugs slightly.

Ellen Everyone had told me the Falls were beautiful. They're not. They're wonderful, but they're not beautiful. I felt myself being pulled down. It frightened me. I thought about Edy and Teddy, and I held myself back.

Irving Thank God.

Ellen But nothing else held me. Nothing.

She's silent.

Irving I'm shocked.

Ellen Why does it surprise you? These last six months, you know nothing of what I'm feeling.

Irving That isn't fair.

Ellen How could you? I'm not blaming you. We have no chance to speak. A puritan society steeped in disapproval forces us to stay in separate hotels. To avoid scandal, they say. All because you're married to a wife you never see. Comfort, forbidden. Closeness, forbidden. In every city in America, we are miles apart. All this adulation has an underside, and the underside is cruel. We must be seen to live as they would wish. Actors are servants of the public, yes. But that's why I never wanted to be an actor.

Irving I had no idea.

Ellen I told you.

Irving Yes. But I did not know how deep your feelings ran.

Loveday appears a long way off, respectful.

Loveday Sir, the crowd is becoming restless. I've given them hooch and pretzels, but I can't keep order much longer.

Irving Tell them I won't be long. I'm unavoidably detained.

Loveday Sir.

Loveday turns and goes.

Ellen I have long ago accepted, Henry, that you are happy in your unhappiness. It suits you. It fits you like a suit. 'It is tragic we cannot be together,' you say. Yes, it is tragic, but for you it is also convenient.

Irving You know the reasons.

Ellen Yes, and I despise them. A stronger man would send your reasons to hell.

Irving I fear Florence's vindictiveness.

Ellen So you say.

Irving Not for myself. I don't fear for myself. I fear for my theatre. Scandal would destroy it utterly.

Ellen And theatre must always come first?

There is a silence.

It was not for you I would have thrown myself into the water. It was for everything.

He moves towards her.

Irving Ellen, you must tell me how I can help you.

Ellen Easy.

Irving How?

Ellen By making me a gift on our return to England.

Irving What gift?

Ellen You know what gift.

He looks at her, distrustful for a moment.

Rosalind.

He says nothing.

We've discussed it.

Irving Yes.

Ellen Before.

Irving A couple of times.

Ellen I'm not tired of supporting roles. Supporting you is the greatest honour of my life.

Irving Thank you.

Ellen I've played many of Shakespeare's women. But I want to play Rosalind.

Irving nods, working out how to play this.

Yes.

Irving I must give it some thought. I must think again. *As You Like It* is not a play I have ever understood. You know my problem with it.

Ellen I know your problem.

Irving Audiences prefer something deeper in the evening.

Ellen You think so?

Irving Something with more meat.

Ellen I disagree. Nobody needs to be told that life is terrible. They know it already. Our job, sometimes, is to give them a source of joy. Tragedy is for people who don't understand life and need it explained to them. Comedy is for those who already know.

Irving stops, hesitating again.

Irving I'm not sure.

Ellen Why not?

Irving Do you really think people will come?

Ellen To see me? As Rosalind?

Irving Now you make me sound insulting, which I don't intend.

Ellen *As You Like It* is the sunniest of all Shakespeare's plays.

Irving I think that may be why I feel so unsuited to producing it.

Ellen It does not have to be you.

There is a silence.

Irving What are you suggesting? Another management?

There is a second silence, this one more profound. Then Irving stirs.

You are right. The travelling is hard. Six months is sufficient. We shall come back but we shall never do more. Agreed?

Ellen Agreed.

Irving Too much soup slopping in our laps in trains. Too much beer. Too many strange beds. Too much false hilarity.

Ellen You hate hilarity.

Irving I like the United States. The cigars are good, and the people are warm. But enough is enough. And if playing Rosalind is the only way to prevent you killing yourself, then you must play Rosalind.

He walks away before she can answer.

Loveday!

He goes out. Ellen is left alone on the empty stage. She looks around her.

Ellen 'Go your ways, go your ways. I knew what you would prove. My friends told me as much, and I thought no less. That flattering tongue of yours won me, 'tis but one cast away, and so come death. By my troth, and in good earnest, and so God mend me, and by all pretty oaths that are not dangerous, if you break one jot of your promise or come one minute behind your hour, I will think you are the most pathetical break-promise and the most hollow lover, and the most unworthy of her you call Rosalind that may be chosen out of the gross band of the unfaithful. Therefore beware my censure and keep your promise.'

From offstage Irving calls for her.

Irving Ellen! Ellen! Where are you?

Ellen I'm coming.

Music. She turns and goes.

End of Act One.

Act Two

13.

Music. Edith comes on with Teddy.

Teddy By the turn of the century our mother was the best-paid woman in England. Not that you'd have known it, because she gave money away like love.

Edith She lost a fortune on Teddy's London seasons.

Teddy I could lose in a week what Ellen made in a year.

Edith The only time I worked with Teddy – on his disastrous production of *The Vikings at Helgeland* – he said that quarrelling with me was not like quarrelling with a woman.

Teddy It's like quarrelling with womanhood itself.

Teddy goes as Edith crosses into the next scene.

14.

The music swells. Outside the medieval house at Smallhythe, a bower on a blissful summer day. Rural heat, greenery. Edith is pacing, tense, wound up. Tony is unmoved, quietly painting the scene on an easel and drinking cider. The year 1926 is projected.

Tony You mustn't worry. She's not going to do it.

Edith How can you be so sure?

Tony I just know.

Edith She's threatening to do it.

Tony She's threatened before.

Edith Yes. But this is worse. Much worse.

Tony Chris is a highly competent woman. She was secretary to Winston Churchill.

Edith Yes.

Tony And to his mother.

Edith In her professional life, yes, Chris is capable. None more so. In her private life, she's a catastrophe.

Edith is suddenly sombre.

And this time it's different.

Tony Different how?

Edith This time it's love.

Tony Love?

Edith Yes. It's love.

Tony is silent for a moment.

Tony And so what was it with you?

Chris appears in gardening clothes, radiating gloom. She sits heavily. Edith and Tony say nothing.

Chris Just so you know . . . both of you . . .

Edith Yes, Chris?

Chris My will is in the desk drawer in my room.

Edith Oh, please!

Chris I'm leaving you everything.

Tony Can I have your eiderdown?

Edith Tony. Please.

There is a short silence.

Chris I've bought a knife. I'm going to cut my wrists.

Edith Chris, I implore you: don't do anything foolish.

Chris I just don't understand.

Edith I know.

Chris I don't understand how she could do this.

Edith It's not that hard.

Chris I can make no sense of her.

Edith You know perfectly well. You always knew. From the moment she first visited Smallhythe, it was obvious. You only have to look at her. Vita Sackville-West is a complex woman. She has complex desires.

Tony Not very, in my experience.

Edith Tony –

Tony She has only one desire and you can spell it in three letters.

A look of rebuke from Edith, but Chris behaves as if she hasn't heard.

Chris How could she do this to me? Vita kissed me in the car –

Tony We know –

Chris She spent the night with me –

Tony We know –

Chris One night. One night only. One wonderful night.

Tony You said.

Chris I didn't even sleep. I lay. I lay drinking her in.

Nobody says anything.

And now – nothing.

Edith Yes.

Chris Not a word.

Edith Yes.

Chris She doesn't want to see me. She never visits. She never answers my letters.

Edith shifts.

Edith Chris, you have to accept it.

Chris Accept what exactly?

Edith Vita's not in love with you.

Chris I'm in love with her.

Edith I understand.

Chris Desperately. I'll die for her.

Edith Yes, but that's not what she wants. She wants you alive and kicking and writing plays and back to your usual abrasive self.

Tony lifts a jug.

Tony Cider?

Chris I'd choke. Why did she sleep with me if she didn't love me?

Tony Well, that's the eternal question, isn't it?

Tony throws Edith a glance to say, 'You deal with this.'

Edith Chris, I'm going to have to explain, I know you're not familiar with this idea –

Chris Go on.

Edith People have different motives at different times.

Chris Obviously.

Tony They're not always in total good faith –

Chris Vita is a wonderful woman –

Edith Maybe. But sometimes people decide that they have to make a judgement. If they are – as Vita was – besieged. You besieged her, Chris. For many months. You pressed yourself upon her. Over and over. You begged.

Chris is genuinely puzzled.

Chris I'm not sure what you're saying.

Edith Sometimes in these circumstances – people give in. Because it's easier. Because they make a calculation. They decide that if they relent, if they offer themselves just once, it may do more to assuage a wound than to inflame it.

Chris looks uncomprehending.

Chris Really?

Edith Yes.

Chris That's how Vita thought? That's why she slept with me?

Tony It was a sympathy frig, for goodness' sake. Even you must know what that is, Chris. You frig but you do it out of pity. We've all done it.

Chris shakes her head.

Chris You're wrong.

Tony Am I?

Chris I swear to God, that's not what this was.

Tony Oh, in the name of goodness, Chris, grow up.

Tony has lost patience. Chris gets up and walks away.

Chris I don't understand. I don't understand who I am. I saw your mother at the Prince's Theatre, Bristol, over thirty years ago and everything became clear to me. A fog of guilt and doubt and confusion lifted, and I saw the ideal of everything a woman could be. I had worshipped her from the stalls. When we met, I couldn't believe that she would take me in and let me look after her.

Edith But she did.

Chris Yes. At that moment, I became myself. I had value. Then the double blessing. Through Ellen, I met you, Edy.

Edith Yes.

Chris And my life changed again. You gave me love.

Edith I hope so.

Chris shakes her head.

Chris Now my life is ruined.

Edith No.

Chris I have no purpose. I have no reason.

Edith You tried to kill yourself once before, Chris.

Chris I remember –

Edith When I was going to marry –

Chris That awful actor –

Edith Yes –

Chris On tour! You wanted to marry Sydney Valentine on tour!

Edith I did –

Tony I must say, Edy, everyone knows, it's the first rule of theatre: never marry on tour.

Chris How could you have dreamt of such a thing?

Edith You were going to kill yourself, Chris. Until my mother prevented it, until Ellen forbade it. And I remained single.

Chris Thank God!

Edith Now here we are, look at us, three contented women of a certain age in the Kentish countryside. What could be better than that?

Chris I'm not contented.

Edith shakes her head.

Edith Think about it, Master Baby. Think. Consider my mother's life –

Chris Your mother?

Edith No, really. What do you think an actor is doing? A producer, an actor, a designer – they're all there to serve. That's all. To serve the play and to serve the company. My mother served the same man for twenty-five years –

Chris She served Henry Irving.

Edith Yes.

Chris Slavishly.

Edith Without complaint. And not always to her own advantage.

Chris Far from it.

Edith And everyone asked if she might have been happier somewhere else. If she'd left the company and done better roles. Wouldn't she have been more fulfilled? Wouldn't she have been more acclaimed? If she'd lived for herself and not for him? They ask over and over. 'Wouldn't she have been greater if she had pursued her own ambitions?' And you know what she would have replied?

Chris I do.

Edith It was her choice. And at the end of it all, she is better known and better loved than any other actress of the age.

Chris Another way of putting it: she served.

Edith Yes.

Chris She was a woman who spent her whole life serving a man.

Edith No. She was an actress.

Chris Oh yes, and tell me, since you so admire service, who exactly did Irving serve?

Edith The theatre.

Chris You think so? I would say, 'The theatre, meaning himself!'

Edith shakes her head, firm now.

Edith No. Chris, let me tell you, because somebody must. I say it from love. You will never find happiness with Vita.

Chris Why not?

Edith Because Vita's wrong for you.

Chris Why?

Edith She's a sybarite, only interested in her own pleasures.

Chris She's a new kind of woman.

Edith Perhaps.

Chris She's liberated.

Edith Vita's morals are contemporary, but her selfishness is ancient. You're unsuited as a couple because you, Chris, are progressive. Vita is not. She never will be. Vita may call herself a feminist, but a feminist who lives only for herself is a nothing. Vita is a tribade who picks people up recklessly and throws them away. And she justifies everything in the name of her feelings. As though feelings trump everything. Really? Vita's feelings exercise a tyranny far more extreme than anything Henry Irving ever attempted. 'I feel this. I feel that.' Who cares? We're not here to feel. We're here to do.

Chris But I have no purpose.

Edith You have a purpose, Chris. You're here to write about my mother, which you do better than anyone, and you're here to write your plays, that's what you're here for. To commemorate Ellen Terry, and to serve the cause of female emancipation. Those two things. Turn your face to the stage.

Chris moves away, helpless.

Chris But I want some happiness.

Edith You have happiness. With Tony and me. And what's more, you make us happy.

Edith looks at Tony to back her up, which she does unconvincingly.

Tony You do.

Chris is standing some way away from them, in agony.

Chris But it's not enough.

15.

Teddy returns to address us directly.

Teddy I admit I saw less and less of Ellen as the years went by. I didn't worry, because she always had Edy, and those two strange friends of hers. My mother seemed fond of the whole set-up.

Even so, Ellen sent me money wherever I was, all over Europe, whenever I needed it. People said it was guilt. But it wasn't. People said I was spoilt. And I wasn't. Because, in truth, it was far simpler than that. Ellen always saw over the hill and beyond. She believed in me.

16.

The sound of torrential applause. Cheering offstage. Then the company of Henry VIII *pass laughing and chattering happily together. Irving passes in costume, elaborately dressed as Cardinal Wolsey in flowing robes, then Ellen made-up to look older as Queen Katherine. Loveday crosses with them, calling out 'Same time tomorrow, company, same time tomorrow!'*

Irving is grim, and walks straight to his dressing room, without speaking. A few moments later, Ellen, in tiara and gown, appears in the familiar room. The year 1892 is projected.

Ellen You left the stage very quickly.

Irving Yes. I had to.

Ellen Why?

Irving Because I had news before the play.

Ellen What sort of news?

Irving I'll tell you in a moment. Sit with me, Ellen. Please.

Ellen Now? I haven't undressed.

Irving I'm asking.

Irving has moved to a bottle of whisky on a shelf and he takes a deep draught from a glass before pouring another, then one for Ellen, who stands, waiting.

Ellen You haven't invited me here for many months.

Irving Is that so?

Ellen No. For many years.

Irving I apologise.

Ellen It was my favourite moment in the day.

Irving Yes. Mine too.

Ellen Why are you asking me now?

Irving doesn't answer.

You seem tired.

Irving I am tired.

Ellen It's strange. We only opened *Henry VIII* last night.

Irving That's right.

Ellen Normally, you'd be full of life.

There is a slight pause.

Irving What do you think?

Ellen What do I think? Of what?

Irving Of the production. You've said nothing.

Ellen I've said nothing because you haven't asked me.

Irving That's remiss. I apologise.

Ellen You no longer ask me anything. And please don't apologise. We know each other far too well for apologies.

Irving waits.

Irving Well?

Ellen My opinion?

Irving Yes.

Ellen Of *Henry VIII*?

Irving Yes.

Ellen Simple. It's one of your greatest triumphs, is it not?

Irving You think so?

Ellen I do.

Irving I'm relieved.

Ellen Cardinal Wolsey plays to your strengths. Episcopal power, worldly power. Is there another actor alive who could play them so well? And the decor . . .

Irving Ah yes, the decor . . .

Ellen The costumes. I doubt if the English stage has ever seen such pictorial grandeur.

Irving So you're pleased?

Ellen Henry, I'm pleased for you.

Irving You're satisfied?

Ellen shifts, exasperated.

Ellen Henry, what do you want me to say?

Irving I want you to tell me the truth.

Ellen You invite me in for the first time in however long. I have no wish to burden you –

Irving Please –

Ellen Since you ask: all right. My life is slipping away. I can feel it. Day by day. And night by night. At the Lyceum. The part of Queen Katherine has not been a challenge. Wolsey carries the play. Spanish queens are hardly a sustaining diet. They live in the margins.

Irving makes a gesture as if to say, 'That's life.'

Look at me. I'm fifty years old and already I'm wearing a white wig. It's unnatural. I arrived with a gift for comedy, and I was at once made into a wife. Now I'm a mother, and pretty soon, no doubt, a grandmother. And where is comedy?

Irving That will change.

Ellen So you keep saying.

Irving You want to talk about repertory now?

Ellen I have no false modesty. The audience greet me with expectation, 'Look, it's Ellen Terry.' And they leave saying, 'I wonder why she did so little tonight.'

Irving We can discuss future roles if that will make you happier.

Ellen is impatient.

Ellen Henry, to be honest, I'm not sure why you've asked me in. What am I doing here? You must have a reason. The only time we are together is on the stage. There, you risk contact. There, you risk warmth. Elsewhere you have become an Arctic of evasion. In the past years, you have come to avoid me everywhere but in a theatre. I find it hard to talk to you when I sense fondness has tapered between us, for reasons not explained to me. Now tell me what it is you wanted to say?

Edith, plainly dressed, looks round the door. She's in her twenties.

Edith Ah, I'm sorry . . .

Irving Not at all –

Edith I was looking for you, Mother.

Ellen Edith, don't worry, Henry and I are just talking.

Edith We're all horrified by your news.

Ellen What news?

Irving Ah. The word is out.

Ellen Word about what?

Edith I'm sorry. Does Ellen not know?

Irving I was about to tell her.

Irving turns to Ellen.

There has been an accident. In Belfast. Laurence is wounded.

Ellen Laurence?

Irving Yes. He's in hospital. But I have been promised he will pull through.

Edith Would you mind if I reassure the company? Rumours are flying.

Irving On the contrary, I'd be grateful.

Edith They will be relieved.

Ellen is frowning, not understanding.

Ellen What's happened? What's happened to your son?

Edith Best you tell my mother in private, sir. I've ordered a cab, Ellen, and there are lamb chops at home waiting to be grilled on the fire.

Ellen Thank you, Edith. Without you, I'd starve.

Edith turns to Irving.

Edith There is not a person in the Lyceum's employ who does not feel for you, Mr Irving. You would not believe the strength of goodwill towards you.

Irving Thank you, Edy. That's kind.

She goes out.

Ellen So now I understand. This is why you called me in.

Irving You're the only person I trust.

Ellen Still? Even now we no longer –

Irving Always.

Ellen waits.

The truth is that Laurence has tried to kill himself. I have this telegram.

He hands a telegram across to Ellen and sits down in his chair.

A bullet passed through his lungs.

Ellen And now?

Irving It's lodged in his back. They're taking it out. They say they have no idea if he'll live.

Ellen What on earth happened? Do you know the reason?

Irving I can guess. Laurence is playing miserably small parts in mirthless comedies. Frank Benson gives him nothing worth playing. Benson thinks he's no good. And meanwhile he's writing horrible plays about the plight of the poor which nobody wants to produce. My son thinks he's born to throw light on injustice and the world is telling him he's not.

Irving shrugs.

Ellen The poor boy. I like him.

Irving We're saying it's an accident. We'll say he was cleaning his gun.

Ellen Laurence carries a gun?

Irving At all times.

Ellen Why?

Irving We'll say it was a prop. We'll say he was preparing for a part.

Ellen frowns.

Ellen And this telegram –

Irving Yes?

Ellen It arrived before the play?

Irving Ten minutes before.

Ellen But that's impossible. I was onstage with you. I saw no sign of your distress.

Irving I should hope not. I tried to give no sign.

Ellen And your son was perhaps fatally wounded.

Irving I was glad of the distraction.

Ellen stares for a moment, taken aback.

Ellen I think I know you, and I don't.

She puts her hand on his back.

How are you feeling, Henry?

Irving I am low, Ellen. I am in despair.

She holds her hand there for a moment, tenderness between them. Then she moves away.

You say we no longer talk after the show.

Ellen Less than we used to.

Irving You know why? Because you see right through me. I can't bear to look at you because you remind me of the life I never led. The other life.

Ellen I offered you that life.

Irving Yes.

Ellen You refused it.

Irving First time we did *Hamlet*, you said, 'Look at the other actors.' That skill I have mastered. In the theatre – yes. But in life – no. Looking at you is far more difficult. And I can't bear to be seen.

There is a silence.

Ellen Laurence is not your fault.

Irving Not entirely, no.

Ellen His mother's to blame.

Irving She's the principal reason, yes. So many times Florence told him not to be an actor. Messing around onstage is not something well-bred people do. The poor boy is torn. Half of him the son of a father he cannot emulate. The other half the son of a snob.

Ellen Have you ever spoken to her? Since the first night of *The Bells*?

Irving We were riding home and Florence asked me when I was going to stop this tomfoolery. I'd just had the greatest triumph of my life. I got out of the cab and closed the door. I've not spoken to her in fifteen years.

Ellen shrugs slightly.

Ellen Perhaps now Laurence's life is in danger, she'll give you a divorce.

Irving I think not. She wants to be Lady Irving. For that at least, the stage might be useful.

Ellen What can you do for Laurence?

Irving Do for him?

Irving looks deep into his whisky glass.

This is the life we live. We pay the price. You as much as me. Look what we've achieved. We took this forsaken art form, both of us, and at the Lyceum we've raised it to a level of influence it has never enjoyed – not since the Elizabethan age. We've made fast progress, but at high expense – men and materiel. Soldiers fall under the wheels. My son has fallen. But we must pick him up.

Ellen Is that all you can say?

Irving What else?

Irving shakes his head. Ellen looks at him, not buying it.

We pick him up.

Ellen I don't understand. I've never understood. Why is influence so important to you?

Irving is disbelieving at the question.

Irving Influence? Surely!

Ellen No, really, I'm asking. Why do you long for the theatre to be at the centre of things?

Irving I would have thought it was obvious.

Ellen No.

Irving It's my whole intention.

Ellen I know. But why?

Irving My goodness, it's everything I've wanted. To make theatre respectable. Respectability is power, and the theatre needs power.

Ellen What for?

Irving So we can survive, so we can build, so we can impose.

Ellen objects.

Ellen We don't do the plays of Ibsen . . .

Irving No –

Ellen We don't do the plays of Shaw –

Irving Certainly not.

Ellen Or of Maeterlinck –

Irving No –

Ellen Strindberg?

Irving None of these.

Ellen Few living writers, nothing about our own world –

Irving No –

Ellen Why not? Too challenging?

Irving Hardly.

Ellen Too difficult? Too threatening to power?

Irving That's not the reason.

Ellen Then what is the reason?

Irving is irritated.

Irving Too small. Too petty. Not large enough.

Ellen Oh really?

Irving Theatre works by metaphor, you know that, Ellen. It works by myth. We're painters, not photographers.

Ellen Exclusively?

Irving People arguing, that isn't theatre. People making points. And what's more, you and I don't belong in drawing rooms. Drawing rooms can't contain us. We need courts and palaces and cathedrals. There's scale for us there. We can move our elbows. Little rooms give us no space.

Ellen We don't do modern plays because they're not right for us?

Irving Just so.

Ellen Is that the only reason?

Irving Big plays suit us. Proper plays with stories. Faust. Macbeth. Philip the Second. Thomas à Becket. These are our people. I'll defend modern writers, but I won't perform them.

Ellen And is that because you fear all your judges and your politicians and your lords don't like that kind of play?

Irving No.

Ellen That kind of play won't go well at Windsor Castle? When we make our annual pilgrimage to perform? Are we stuck forever with patriotic myth? Do you never long for a theatre a little rougher than that?

Irving stares at her.

It's what Laurence wants, isn't it? Something less pompous? Something less grand?

Irving Yes. But he lacks the skill. That's why he's in hospital with a bullet in his back.

Irving looks into his whisky, deeply unhappy. Ellen gets up to go. Then she turns at the door.

Ellen To you, the theatre is everything, Henry. To me, it's nothing. I'd rather be a successful human being. You fear losing the Lyceum. I don't.

Irving So what do you fear?

Ellen Truthfully? The only thing I fear is the dwindling of love.

17.

Music. Edith comes back to address us, as behind her, the scene is dramatically changed.

Edith All my life I followed the path of reason. My brother followed the path of intuition. Inconsistency never bothered him for a moment. On the one hand, Henry Irving and Ellen Terry were the greatest practitioners the theatre had ever known. On the other hand, everything they had done had to be swept away. And Teddy was born to do the sweeping.

How many plays did Teddy produce in exile? Three. One in Germany, one in Italy, and one in Russia. The last one was *Hamlet* – for Stanislavski. He said for him *Hamlet* wasn't a play. *Hamlet* was the story of his life.

18.

Hamlet again. The year 1912 is projected. It could not be more different from the previous. This time, Claudius and Gertrude are sitting high above the stage with an enormous golden cloak flowing down to the floor, where Hamlet sits brooding in a trap. All the other courtiers have their faces sticking out of slits in the golden pyramid of cloth. It is as if the whole court is nothing but a projection of Hamlet's own fantasy. There are dramatic shafts of light to create a phantasmagorical world. The same scene Irving rehearsed, but this time it's all in Russian.

Hamlet (*Russian*) 'Madam, how like you this play?'

Gertrude (*Russian*) 'The lady doth protest too much, methinks.'

Hamlet (*Russian*) 'O but she'll keep her word . . .'

Claudius (*Russian*) 'Have you heard the argument? Is there no offence in't?'

Hamlet (*Russian*) 'No, no, they do but jest, poison in jest . . .'

Teddy climbs onto the stage, in a towering rage, to end the proceedings.

Teddy No, no, this is terrible, this is not what I wanted. Why can nobody do what I want?

The actors stop, well used to this. Stage managers run on, and among the rush of activity is Konstantin Stanislavski, tall, dignified, at this point aged forty-nine, and Leopold Sulerzhitsky, forty, known as Suler, smaller, compact. They speak accented English.

Stanislavski Please tell us what is the problem?

Teddy Get rid of Suler. I can't work with him.

Stanislavski Suler is helping you. He's your assistant.

Teddy He's out to destroy my production. He's destroying it completely. Oh my God, this is why I never produce.

Suler is standing, uncomprehending. One or two of the actors struggle out from under the huge robe.

Suler It's just as it was. Everything's the same.

Teddy Exactly!

Suler Yesterday you were happy.

Teddy I was happy yesterday. It was good yesterday. Today it is not. Gertrude's not looking at Claudius.

Suler That's what you asked for!

Teddy She's looking out front! It has to keep changing, or how does it breathe? You always keep it the same. That's not theatre.

Teddy is shouting.

Stanislavski Shall we all take a break?

The stage manager shouts out – surtitles – 'Ten minutes, everyone, we take ten minutes!' The weary actors begin to go off. The stage lights change to rehearsal lights.

Teddy I have a vision. Suler doesn't understand it.

Stanislavski He's a famous director in his own right.

Teddy I demand you take Suler's name off the programme.

Stanislavski That's hardly the most important question right now.

Suler I don't care! Take it off!

Stanislavski What does it matter?

Teddy But it does, don't you see? It matters more than anything. Everyone has been waiting for me to do a production. Europe is holding its breath. Finally! At last!

The *Hamlet* of Edward Gordon Craig! At the Moscow Art! For Stanislavsky!

Stanislavski is calm, reasonable.

Stanislavski We've given you all the facilities –

Teddy I accept that –

Stanislavski We've given you the money, we've given you the company –

Teddy You have –

Stanislavski We've given you the time –

Teddy Not enough time!

Stanislavski You've worked for three years. We've paid you. Only the Moscow Art Theatre could contemplate doing such a thing.

Teddy I should never have done this, I should never have produced. It was a mistake.

Teddy walks away. Stanislavski turns in despair to Suler. Surtitles are projected.

Stanislavski (*Russian*) Could you get us some tea?

Suler (*Russian*) I'm happy to. He's impossible. He's a spoilt child.

Suler goes out. Teddy's mood has changed. Downstage, by himself, he's sulky.

Teddy All right, I admit, it's my fault.

Stanislavski No one's at fault.

Teddy No, really. I should never have become involved in production. Theory's far more important.

Stanislavski Possibly.

Teddy I was so happy editing my magazine. Writing about what theatre should be. That's far more interesting than doing it. Anyone can do it. That's the easy part.

Stanislavski At the Moscow Art Theatre, you'll understand, that's not how we feel.

Teddy Even so. In an ideal world we wouldn't even open. If a work of art is to be legendary, it's important that almost nobody sees it.

Teddy looks at him, suddenly warm and kind.

Shall I tell you my real problem with theatre? Why it can never be fulfilling?

Stanislavski Please do.

Teddy Once you do something, then it's not everything.

Stanislavski thinks this over.

Stanislavski Yes. Yes, that's a problem.

Teddy It is.

Stanislavski I can see.

Teddy It's just something. It opens. It's just another play. It drives me crazy. The moment I commit to an image, I am saying no to a different image.

Stanislavski Yes, inevitably.

Teddy It's so damned limiting. How can you stand it? In my imagination, it's infinite. But in realisation, it's nothing!

Stanislavski I've heard this before. This disappointment. My friend Chekhov said this all the time.

But Teddy has already turned and is gesturing at the abandoned set.

Teddy Just look at this. My *Hamlet*. It was going to be great. Shakespeare believes in the supernatural. *Hamlet*'s first scene is with a ghost. Honestly, if you don't believe in the supernatural, don't even attempt Shakespeare. Don't go near him.

Stanislavski It will be great. We believe in you. We believe in your genius.

Teddy Konstantin, you're a very good friend.

Teddy goes over and hugs him. He's almost apologetic.

For me, the programme is vital.

Stanislavski I know.

Teddy It must say I produced *Hamlet* alone. I have very few achievements, but I have a great reputation. That reputation must not be threatened.

Stanislavski I'll get Suler to agree.

Teddy He's a good man.

Stanislavski He is.

Teddy Underneath.

Teddy looks at Stanislavski, regretful.

People who don't like me call me a charlatan. I'm not. I'm an inspiration. People will speak of me for years. My name will live longer than those who just put on plays.

Teddy smiles, self-satirising.

'Edward Gordon Craig, what a shame the theatre business had no use for him.' That's what they'll say. But you and I know my secret.

Stanislavski What is your secret? Truly?

Teddy I don't want to have a use.

They both smile. Stanislavski is deeply moved.

Stanislavski You're a funny man.

Teddy Now let's get this bloody thing moving. What are we doing? I hate waiting around.

Suler has reappeared with glasses of tea. The actors return to assume their places.

I've no time for tea. I'm far too busy. I'm wondering if this gold cloak idea is going to work. I liked it yesterday, now I'm not sure. If only we could get the shadows deeper. And the gold should be golder. And there's something wrong with the fall of the material. Are you sure we made it in the right stuff? Would it be better in linen? Or maybe Claudius and Gertrude in different materials? Contrast? Competing colours? Did you know I was the first designer ever to use hessian in the theatre? Did you know that? No? Shall we rip up what we've got and start again? Shall we?

He turns, perfectly cheerful, to Stanislavski and Suler, who stand amazed.

So tell me, gentlemen, what do you think?

19.

Music. Hamlet *disappears and is replaced by a group of three businessmen, the Comyns Carr brothers, in Victorian frockcoats, sitting at a card table with Irving. He is much older and weaker.*

Meanwhile, Edith appears to address us directly.

Edith I didn't mind being neglected. No, really. It disturbed me not at all. The English theatre shut me out. Urgency is one thing, they said – all that stuff about women – yes. But what about style? Behind their hands, they said I didn't meet their standards. Whenever artistic people talk about standards, what they really mean is doing it the same as them.

They couldn't hurt me. Believe me, they tried. The brightest flowers sometimes bloom in darkened meadows, not transited. And sometimes they die without being seen.

20.

Music swells. Café Royal. Ellen is sitting downstage at a white-clothed table, waiting patiently while the men inaudibly discuss business upstage. Finally, they all shake hands. Then they audibly laugh. Only Irving seems grave. Ellen sits, not moving, knowing what's happening. The year 1899 is projected. Then Irving is heard to say 'Gentlemen' as he leaves to join Ellen.

Ellen And so. You've done it.

Irving nods.

You're selling the Lyceum.

Irving Not selling, no. Floating it as a viable business.

Ellen They're buying you?

Irving I'm attracting investors. Yes.

Irving sits down at the table beside her.

Ellen On what terms?

Irving The theatre is theirs. I'm back on a salary.

Ellen And what promises have you made in return?

Irving To appear.

Ellen In your own theatre?

Irving In what was my own theatre.

Ellen How often?

Irving Personally?

Ellen Yes.

Irving I must appear on the stage a hundred times a year.

Ellen A hundred?

Irving Yes. And I must do four months of touring.

Ellen 'Must'?

Irving In return for them taking on my debts.

Ellen And do they feel that's what you're worth?

A Waiter appears in a long white apron.

Irving I'll have a brandy and soda.

Waiter Miss Terry?

Ellen Nothing for me.

The Waiter goes.

Irving They're appointing me Artistic Advisor.

Ellen That's grand of them. Do you get to advise on repertory?

Irving Yes. No new productions, I'm afraid. They won't pay for them.

Ellen You'll revive old favourites?

Irving Just for the moment.

Ellen Spare us *The Bells*.

Irving Yes, *The Bells*.

Irving looks miserable.

I fear there are bound to be cutbacks.

Ellen Cutbacks?

Irving Yes. They say that I've been too extravagant. Too many people on stage.

Ellen Ah yes. Too many actors?

Irving And also too many staff.

Ellen Where? Front of house? In the bars?

Irving Everywhere.

Ellen In the wardrobe? Backstage?

Irving They're going to put in managers to make the theatre more efficient.

Ellen I'm sure the audience will love that. They will leave the theatre, ablaze with excitement. 'That was wonderful. It was so efficient.'

Irving is reproachful, picking up her tone.

Irving Ellen, I know how you feel.

Ellen Do you?

Irving But these people have a point. It's true, I was wasteful. I spent too much money on parties.

Ellen The parties were part of it.

Irving Ellen, last season lost ten thousand pounds. I couldn't go on. And the fire destroying all the scenery –

Ellen I know your reasons –

Irving Well? Do you think I had any choice?

Ellen We always have a choice.

The Waiter comes back with the brandy and soda.

Irving Thank you.

Waiter Are you sure, Miss Terry?

Ellen I need nothing.

Waiter I wish you would have something. Forgive me. It's always been my ambition to say I served Ellen Terry.

Ellen looks up at him, moved.

Ellen Then bring me whatever you think I might like.

Waiter Thank you.

The Waiter smiles and goes out.

Irving I don't know what other course I could have taken.

Ellen You know very well.

Irving Do I?

Ellen You do. You know what Bernard Shaw is proposing –

Irving Oh, Shaw!

Ellen Well?

Irving I don't like Bernard Shaw. A National Theatre!

Ellen Yes! A group of eminent practitioners, under your leadership, getting together to found a theatre for the advancement of the form. Taking the business out of the business. This is the moment, and you are the man.

Irving looks down, grumbling.

Irving I can't think why. The scoundrel's always despised me.

Ellen His taste is different, that's all.

Irving Shaw thinks I'm old-fashioned.

Ellen Henry, you know full well that isn't the point!

Ellen has uncharacteristically raised her voice in exasperation.

You're a towering figure. He knows that. You're the only man in England who can take on the job. Every soul in that theatre has given you loyalty. Do they not deserve a measure of loyalty in return? You are planning to betray everyone who works for you. The people who sweep the stage as much as the people who parade across it.

And betray them in the most profound way possible. By destroying their dreams. You think a theatre's just the person who leads it? It isn't. You are as beholden to the staff as the staff are to you.

Irving I know that.

Ellen Do you have any idea how ardently they've supported you? Working through the night and then two hours' sleep? For no other reason but that they believed in you. And not just in you. Not just the man. The idea. The idea of a high-aiming theatre that isn't just commerce and bilge. And these are the people you now propose to throw in the gutter.

Irving Do you think I haven't considered them? Do you think their redundancy doesn't keep me awake?

He looks at her resentfully.

I'm exhausted, Ellen. Look at me. The natural life of a theatre company is – what? Five years? Eight? I've been running the Lyceum for over twenty.

Ellen And you can run it another twenty!

Irving Are you mad? My health won't stand it. I've had pneumonia.

Ellen It's just an excuse.

Irving I've had bronchitis. And pleurisy.

She looks scornful.

Ellen I've always believed in the best of you, Henry. The best Henry Irving. And I've held you to it, whenever I could. This time, when they brought me the rumours, I refused to believe them. Not Henry, I said. Henry would never sell the Lyceum. It's his life. He would never do it.

Irving I have to do it.

Ellen Can you sit here, now, in the Café Royal, and tell me you intend to destroy what you created? Can you?

Irving I've signed the contract.

Ellen In cold blood? And you're at peace, are you, with letting us down?

Irving And presumably by 'us', you really mean 'you'.

The Waiter returns with a loaded tray.

Waiter There's a hot chocolate. And there's a brandy. There's also a rum. And a beer. To be safe. A beef and horseradish sandwich.

Ellen Thank you.

Waiter I added some oysters. And half a lobster. I fear I may have overdone it.

Ellen I'm sure not.

Waiter Just leave whatever you don't want.

Ellen I shall.

Waiter It's from the management. They said it would be an honour.

Ellen Thank you. That's very kind.

Waiter Let us know if you need anything more.

The Waiter goes. Ellen looks at the array. She lifts a fork, but goes no further.

Irving You should eat.

Ellen I don't think I can.

Irving nods, and takes the brandy.

Irving I acknowledge your view. Of course I do. I shall give you all the time you need.

Ellen Time for what?

Irving Obviously. To decide. Whether your own position is untenable.

Ellen My position?

Irving Yes.

Ellen And what position is that?

Irving Leading lady.

Ellen changes, understanding his purpose.

Ellen Oh I see. And is this what this is about? Is this what I'm doing here? This meeting? Is that why you've taken me out? Not to consult but to dismiss? Am I surplus to the business's new requirements? Do I look untidy on the balance sheet?

Irving Far from it.

Ellen Well then?

Irving You are the Lyceum. You as much as me.

Irving shifts.

But I did foresee that the new arrangements would distress you.

Ellen Yet you went ahead with them.

Irving Ellen, please. I had to make a judgement in everyone's interest. I weighed you as a significant factor.

Ellen I obviously don't weigh very heavily.

Irving We want you to stay. Everyone wants you to stay. But nobody wants to force you if you're unhappy.

Ellen And what would be your own wish?

Irving You know what I want.

Ellen I'd like to hear you say it.

There is a short silence.

Irving Ellen, all my life I have sought fulfilment through art. I was a poor actor until I was forty. I knew it and

I was determined to improve. The knowledge of my own inadequacy infected my every step, my every breath. I achieved twenty years of professional work in a continuous agony of self-consciousness. You were the instrument of my transformation. You changed me completely and for all time. Together we made a harmony we could not make apart. When I am in a play without you, I look around and the stage is empty. But you have also endowed me with the strength to continue alone. If I must. But only if I must. Thanks to you, I am good enough.

Ellen looks a moment, moved.

Ellen All right, you say you don't want me unhappy. But you know perfectly well: I've never put a high price on happiness. We both know you're making a mistake. You're squandering the chance to create something original and great. But my feelings are not important. Loyalty and feeling are something different. My loyalty's with you. It always has been. And not as an actor, either. No. What matters to me is whether I will be of some use to you in this rickety and misguided venture.

Irving You'll be of some use.

Ellen Very well then. I aim to continue. For as long as you need me.

Irving I need you.

Ellen Thank you. I needed to be sure. Let's make the great mistake together.

Irving reaches out his hand and puts it on hers.

I'm peckish. Maybe the lobster?

She pushes the plate inches towards him, but Irving shakes his head.

Henry? Maybe the beef?

21.

Music. Teddy appears to address us. The year 1966 is projected.

Teddy In 1911, I published my manifesto *On the Art of the Theatre*. It's a great classic. As far as I know, it's never been out of print.

Now I spend most of the day playing patience in Saint-Paul-de-Vence. Sixty theatre practitioners, who call themselves The Friends of Edward Gordon Craig, have clubbed together. They send me one hundred pounds a month from their own pockets as a way of saying thank you for existing. I rise with the sun, and I live well enough.

Chief among them is a young man called Peter Brook. He comes to pay homage. Half-Russian, I think. He says he owes everything to me. Turns out he's a fellow enemy of realism. I said, 'Good luck, Peter. Do well.'

22.

Ellen, dressed for the street and carrying a bunch of yellow daffodils, come up the stairs to a spacious hotel room. Then she goes in. Irving is in bed, grey with age and illness, his dressing gown falling off him. He looks like an old tree. He is drinking coffee. The year 1905 is projected.

Irving Ah, what a pleasure to see Ellen Terry in Wolverhampton.

Ellen We toured here often, remember.

Irving How could I forget? Always a graveyard for the drama.

Ellen Binding theatrical lore: East Midlands for comedy, West Midlands for tragedy.

Irving True. I've never got a laugh west of Nottingham.

Ellen But when you acted with me, at least you managed to stay upright.

Irving It's nothing. I'm recovering.

Ellen I can see.

Irving And there is no better medicine than you being here.

She takes a simple vase out of her bag.

Ellen I brought you daffodils. And a vase. Because I knew what the hotel vase would be like.

Irving You prefer plain.

Ellen Always. In fact, when I went to the florist, they only had lilies. I told them white flowers are for funerals.

Irving No white flowers, then.

She arranges the flowers in the vase.

I tripped.

Ellen Sorry?

Irving That's what happened.

Ellen Ah.

Irving Yes. It was that rug in front of the door. A commercial traveller picked me up. Kind of him, but then the damn fellow wouldn't stop talking.

Ellen Really?

Irving All sorts of professional questions.

Ellen What kind?

Irving You know. The kind civilians ask. How do we remember the lines?

Ellen Ah.

Irving Is it true that Ellen Terry convulses with laughter so badly that on occasions she has to depart the stage before the end of the scene?

Ellen My reputation goes before me.

Irving And, of course, how I manage to go white when I hear the bells?

Ellen It's a good question. How do you manage to go white?

Irving I really don't know.

Ellen Well I do. You act so intensely that your heart drains.

Irving You think so?

Ellen Yes. I'm sure of it. And then your face discolours.

Irving Huh.

Ellen You've been doing it for over twenty years. You've been killing yourself.

Irving looks at her as if thinking it over.

Irving The doctor wants me to rest for eight weeks. I shan't, of course.

Ellen Why not?

Irving Because he thinks it's my heart. But he's wrong. It's my breath. I took a tumble, that's all. He says if I stop acting, I might have ten years.

Ellen And if you continue?

Irving Fewer.

Ellen So what will you do?

Irving Continue. Things as they are, I have to tour.

Ellen You mean since the Lyceum went bust?

Irving Yes.

Ellen Under that disastrous new management?

Irving You never cared for them, did you?

Ellen I warned you.

Irving I heard your warning.

Ellen And you chose not to heed it.

Irving Does it give you satisfaction to be proved right?

Ellen No. Not at your expense. Never at your expense.

Irving You've been right a few times.

Ellen Yes.

Irving And so have I.

There is a moment between them.

Ellen And here you are, endlessly traversing the kingdom. Today Aberdeen, tomorrow Penzance. Yet another farewell tour.

Irving I try to offer farewell tours at yearly intervals. People expect them. Goodbye, Brighton. Goodbye, Billingham. I feel I should have a carriage and wave. They're putting me in the Abbey, you know. When the time comes.

Ellen I shall tread all over you.

Irving I would like that.

She smiles at him.

Ellen You've had a wonderful life, haven't you?

Irving Oh yes. A wonderful life. Of work. And there's nothing better, after all, is there?

Ellen I don't know, Henry.

Irving You'd have liked to find out?

Ellen I'd like to have been given the chance.

Irving Give me your hand.

She holds it out and he kisses it.

We were happy together, weren't we?

Ellen Always.

Irving Disagreement is fruitful, don't you think?

Ellen Intensely fruitful. And enjoyable. If I had to spend my life arguing with anyone, it would be with you.

Irving But you have, haven't you?

Ellen I've tried.

Irving They tell me you have a new husband, is that right? Always up for an adventure, that's Ellen. What is he, the third?

Ellen He was.

Irving 'Was'? Does that mean dispatched already?

Ellen He's gone the way of the others, yes.

Irving They do slip through your fingers, don't they, Nell?

She looks at him a moment.

Ellen And the end, Henry, the end. How would you like that to come?

Irving thinks for a few moments. Then he snaps his fingers, the action before the words.

Irving Like that!

They look at each other. Then:

Not that I'm anywhere near it, of course.

Ellen Of course.

Irving The advantage of performing in the classics. I've done a lot of death scenes. I know how to play them by now. Death won't catch me unawares.

He smiles.

Ellen I'm going back to London.

Irving It was kind of you to come. There was no need.

Ellen There was every need.

Irving If you come back in a week, you will find me onstage.

Ellen I hope not.

Irving It's my intention.

Ellen What will you do?

Irving What I always do.

Ellen Revive *The Bells*?

Irving Yes. And if you do come back, please be sure to assist me afterwards with any helpful observations you may have on my performance. I'm sure I shall profit from them.

Ellen I shall do my best.

Irving Frustrating, isn't it? Lately I feel I'm just beginning to get the hang of the acting.

They both smile.

Ellen And by the way, I still want to play Rosalind. She's the only one I haven't played. I really wanted to play her.

Irving I know.

Ellen You promised me.

Irving Yes.

Ellen And then you never let me.

Irving No. You've lived her.

Ellen Yes. But I haven't played her. I can't remember why.

There is a silence.

Irving No. Nor can I.

Ellen steps out of the hotel room to address us directly.

Ellen Henry played *The Bells* again only once, and within hours of defying doctors' orders and dying onstage in his most famous role, died offstage as himself. They brought me the news in Manchester. A play called *Alice Sit-by-the-Fire*. Henry would have wished me to go on that night. But when I reached the lines 'It's summer done, autumn begun. I had a beautiful husband once, black as the raven was his hair', I broke down and the audience went home.

Irving appears as a ghost behind Ellen, still young, speaking lines from Henry VIII.

Irving 'This is the state of man: today he puts forth
The tender leaves of hopes: tomorrow blossoms,
And bears his blushing honours thick upon him;
The third day comes a frost, a killing frost,
And when he thinks, good easy man, full surely
His greatness is a-ripening, nips his root,
And then he falls, as I do.'

Ellen It was in another provincial hotel. People said it was not a suitable ending. A great man like Irving should have died in his bed, surrounded by family and friends. I felt the opposite. The lobby of the Midland, Bradford, dead on the foyer floor, seemed to me entirely appropriate.

He belonged to England, and he gave himself back.

Irving 'There is betwixt that smile we would aspire to,
That sweet aspect of princes, and their ruin
More pangs and fears than wars and women have;
And when he falls, he falls like Lucifer,
Never to hope again.'

The light on Irving goes to darkness.

Ellen They asked me to go up to Yorkshire to see him. I said there was no point. Why would I? He was no longer there.

The sound of laughter and applause coming from the Barn Theatre in Smallhythe. Ellen goes out. Tony is sitting outside in the sunshine, painting as usual. She is much older. The year 1928 is projected. Chris, also much older, appears from the cottage.

Chris Can I bring her out?

Tony No. You know the problem. Wait for the audience to leave. If we bring her out too early.

Chris This place has turned into a shrine.

Edith appears and there are three elderly, grey-haired ladies on a country lawn.

Edith She's getting restless.

Chris We have to bring her out.

Edith I don't want people to see her. It isn't right.

Chris She wouldn't mind. She's hardy.

Edith I'm not thinking about her. I'm thinking about my actors. It's not right that they should work so hard, then find themselves in her shade.

Tony It's hard to explain to her, 'You can't come out because everyone will stare.'

The sound of applause from the Barn Theatre.

Edith How's the play going, Master Baby?

Chris It's rip-roaring. The audience love it. They love a call to feminine violence.

Tony Then they go home and make tea for their husbands.

Chris Tony, you don't know that for sure.

Tony I'm guessing.

Edith Ellen would hate it.

Chris Again, are you sure?

Edith My mother has one weakness. She won't pick a side. She always wants to reconcile.

Tony Is that weakness?

Edith Spoken from the heart.

Edith leans over and kisses Tony's forehead. From across the garden, the sound of cheering and of the Barn doors being flung open.

Chris That must be the end. They love it. They always go for it. Women to the barricades, and off we go!

Tony Hurrah!

Chris At least this year there's something to celebrate.

Edith What?

Chris Finally winning the vote!

Edith Oh yes.

Chris turns back, watching the crowd go.

Chris There they are, pouring out into the orchard, God bless them, chattering among themselves and ready for the fight. Good luck to them.

Edith So can we bring her out?

Chris Why not? They're heading towards the road.

Tony Then bring her out.

Edith goes off towards the house. Tony and Chris are left alone.

Chris Do you think she has long?

Tony Who?

Chris Ellen.

Tony No. Not long.

Edith reappears pushing her mother in a bathchair. Ellen is eighty-two, and transformed, near blind, her hair wild and Pre-Raphaelite, like a mad woman, with a blanket over her. Her voice is thinner, but powerful as ever.

Ellen And let me tell you one more thing . . .

Edith A moment, Mother.

Ellen What happened. Ask me what happened.

Edith What happened, Mother?

Ellen When we got to America.

Edith You were always going to America.

Ellen I enjoyed the voyage. You're powerless. You're stuck on a boat and nothing's your fault. I liked that.

Edith I can't think why.

Ellen And they understood us in America. Warm people. Warm but a little lost.

She has stopped.

Edith So what happened, Mother?

Ellen They asked Henry, 'To what do you attribute your success?'

Edith And what did he reply?

Ellen 'To my acting.'

There is a silence, no one knowing what to say.

'To my acting.' Isn't that perfect?

Edith Yes. Can I get you anything?

Ellen No.

Edith has arranged the chair in the sun and now sits down next to her. Tony paints on. Chris watches.

So the first thing that's going to happen is that we'll be reunited.

Edith When?

Ellen If there's something called heaven. No heaven unless Henry is there. Being impossible.

Edith has a book.

Edith Would you like me to read to you, Mother?

Ellen No, thank you, Edith. I've got so used to nurses reading badly, good reading would be so odd. I couldn't stand the shock.

Edith I can read badly if you like.

Ellen You could never read badly, Edith.

Edith is taken aback by this unusual warmth.

People don't understand rhythm, and they don't understand emphasis. They don't understand secrecy. Watch Henry. He makes you want to know what he knows, but he makes you work for it.

She smiles a moment.

I find with reality nowadays –

Edith Reality, Mother?

Ellen Yes. Sometimes nowadays reality falls off a cliff. And at other times it sails.

Edith Sails where, Mother?

Ellen Into the distance.

She looks away.

I never knew him, really. Not really. Didn't really know him.

Then she smiles to herself.

My sister was the talented one, not me. Life's hard, but it's harder when you're stupid.

Tony gets up.

Tony I'm going in to make supper. Is there anything you want?

Ellen I could look some haddock in the eye.

Tony There's some in the larder.

Ellen I want it. In milk.

Tony Yes.

Ellen Warmed.

Tony goes out.

I heard people in the garden.

Edith That was the audience.

Ellen We have a theatre?

Edith Yes.

Ellen How wonderful. What a good idea.

Chris waits a moment.

Chris Will you sit with her till supper?

Edith Yes.

Chris I can stay in the garden if you like.

Edith No. We'll be fine.

Chris Well then.

Chris goes out. Edith and her mother are alone. Evening comes down. The leaves are heard to rustle in a summer wind, Ellen's eyes are closed.

Edith Leave Ellen Terry out in the sun.